The Graphic Facilitator's Guide:

How to use your listening, thinking & drawing skills to make meaning

Brandy Agerbeck

 loosetooth.com library

Loosetooth.com Library

First published 2012

ISBN: 0615591876
ISBN-13: 978-0615591872

Cover design by Brandy Agerbeck
Edited by Jenni Grover Prokopy
Typesetting by Brandy Agerbeck, set in Franklin Gothic

Photo credits:
Guido Neuland © 2010-2011, pages 94, 157, 207, 236, 279
Jamie Nast © 2012 page 228

Find more resources at **GraphicFacilitator.com**

The Graphic Facilitator's Guide

How to use your listening, thinking & drawing skills to make meaning

Brandy Agerbeck

Table of Contents

When people ask me, "So what do you do?" I say, "I've got a really strange job. I'm a graphic facilitator."

[Cue sound of crickets.]

Once I describe what the heck that means, folks are intrigued. It took me seven years of doing the work before I understood how to clearly answer the question. Another seven years later, I'm ready to share this guide with you. I welcome you into the next wave of graphic facilitators tackling that question.

This book focuses on the specific role of mapping a meeting with words and images. The work is a powerful tool for groups to be more productive. Even more powerful are the abilities of listening, thinking and drawing that fuel graphic facilitation. Acuity in these skills holds a much broader power. I invite you to develop your powers by focusing on this role first.

In a few pages, we'll begin answering the question, "What is a graphic facilitator?" First, let me share some thanks.

My deepest thanks go to my dear colleagues John Ward and Lynn Carruthers. At my second International Forum of Visual Practitioners (IFVP) conference, John approached me and said, "I like you so much, I now consider you my sister." I couldn't be prouder to be John's adopted sibling. Our umpteen conversations about drawing over the past decade have fed my mind and soul. Please check out his kinesthetic modeling process for just a peek into his magnificent mind.

Lynn Carruthers is a force of nature and my most trusted sounding board. In 2005, Lynn asked, "What if you and I did the beginners class at next year's IFVP conference?" That wonderful "what if" became a great three-year collaboration and co-teaching experience with Lynn. I thank her for pushing me into organizing my thoughts about this work and letting me go nuts with the class workbook. The three iterations of that workbook were the roots of this guide. Lynn's candor and kindness have meant the world to me.

Thank you to Sari Gluckin and Pamela Meyer both of whom are clients, collaborators and friends. I've had the great pleasure of working with both women for a dozen years, and the longevity of our working relationships has taught me heaps.

Sari is a master of posing the perfect generative question and infusing her facilitation with design thinking. She has gifted me countless opportunities to map the meetings of her clients. Our seamless process allows us to leave sentences unfinished and we can communicate with knowing nods. That ease belies all the good work and thinking we've shared around facilitating groups to wish when they think. I thank Sari for sharing her practice with me so I could strengthen mine.

Pamela Meyer is a wonderful role model in treating every person and interaction with thoughtfulness and integrity. She fuses focus with playfulness, teaching people how to turn workplaces into playspaces. We had a fantastic first adventure in self-publishing when we co-created our book *Permission: A Guide to Generating More Ideas, Being More of Yourself and Having More Fun at Work* (Playspace Press, 2011). In the midst of laying out that book, I traveled to New Zealand. One morning, I had an ultra-vivid dream that I was creating a book about **The Essential Eight** in *Permission's* format. Upon waking, I knew my next project. Seven months later, here is that dream come to life.

On the home front, a big bear hug to my partner Scott Forschler. He's the non-visual philosopher and I'm the non-philosophical artist, but we share curiosity, our love of learning, and of thinking about thinking. Scott's sweetness and stability has been a most positive emotional tether to help keep me grounded before I flew away or flamed out.

Looking to the past, I am grateful that I stumbled into Grinnell College. I had no idea what college really meant, but I had an intuitive pull to that tiny, intense campus in the middle of Iowa. Grinnell was the perfect environment to foster my critical thinking and independence. Thank you to Jim, Aaron, Ross,

Amihan, Dan, Gwen, Shea, Kathleen and many others for their enduring friendships. Much love to my dearest friend Rebecca Kresse, who reminds me that life is too short, but I'll always remember her heart and how she shone.

Thank you to MG Taylor Corporation for the incredible window into how people work together, both our teams and our clients. After wandering out of Grinnell, classmate Kathy Clemons helped me stumble into an Ernst and Young office that used MG Taylor's processes. I discovered that my love of drawing and thinking had the name of graphic facilitation, and what the heck a "knowledge worker" was. My three most important lessons were iteration, documenting your process, and how to form teams for the task at hand.

I know I'm so darn full of thanks, but I'd also like to thank my editor Jenni Grover Prokopy. We started out as friends of friends who both happened to be expanding our businesses in the same directions. I thank Jenni for her compassion, camaraderie and editing to make this book stronger.

I thank **you** for taking the time to read this book. I hope it enables you to do great things and facilitate others in doing great things.

Last, I want to share a quote that gives me chills. It is from architect and urban planner Daniel Burnham. When I first read this quote, it connected to my love of Chicago:

Make no little plans. They have no magic to stir men's blood and probably themselves will not be realized. Make big plans; aim high in hope and work, remembering that a noble, logical diagram once recorded will never die, but long after we are gone will be a living thing, asserting itself with ever-growing insistency. Remember that our sons and grandsons are going to do things that would stagger us. Let your watchword be order and your beacon beauty. Think big.

Daniel Burnham
Chicago architect
1846-1912

Years later, I reread the quote and it bowled me over with how it resonates with my work as a graphic facilitator. One hundred plus years after this was written, let's stir women's blood too, and explicitly add the daughters and granddaughters.

Let us realize our big plans through our noble, logical diagrams. I hope these pages help you seek both order and beauty in your work.

Graphic Facilitation Success Factors

Before we dive in, here's a list of qualities that lead to success in graphic facilitation. Mark all that apply to you.

- [ ] You have a black belt in listening.

- [ ] When you're talking to someone, you often stop and summarize: "So, what I hear you saying is..." The person agrees with your summary.

- [ ] You have legible penmanship.

- [ ] You are brave and will stand in front of a group and draw/write.

- [ ] You put your own needs aside to serve the group as a whole.

- [ ] You have design experience and understand composition and how to use placement, color and scale to organize information.

- [ ] You can listen objectively with "outsider ears" even if you have a personal investment in the conversation.

- [ ] You are never or rarely told, "You are not listening to me."

- [ ] You can draw or will learn to draw.

- [ ] If you already draw well, you are a fast drawer.
- [ ] If you already draw, you don't fall in love with your drawings.
- [ ] You want to serve others.
- [ ] You are good at making connections between things.
- [ ] You tend to see the big picture.
- [ ] You see how pieces fit together into a whole.
- [ ] You enjoy thinking about how ideas are organized.
- [ ] You learn with your hands.
- [ ] You listen better if you're writing or drawing.
- [ ] You like working with your whole body.
- [ ] You can focus on a conversation and feel "in" it.
- [ ] You are able to multitask. The idea of listening, organizing and drawing at the same time doesn't short-circuit your brain.
- [ ] You spell well.
- [ ] You're not freaked out by the thought of misspelling in front of people.
- [ ] You see patterns emerge.

- [ ] You seek out the commonalities between people, ideas and things.

- [ ] You want meetings to be productive, and to never waste anyone's time.

- [ ] You are good at reading group dynamics.

- [ ] You work well in a changing, dynamic environment.

- [ ] You adapt well to changes.

- [ ] You are self-directed.

- [ ] You are independent.

- [ ] You are self-aware and know how to challenge yourself.

- [ ] You are good at inferring things and figuring things out in context.

The more of these qualities you've marked, the more likely you'll be attracted to and succeed in this work. Many of these skills can be learned and attitudes developed. Throughout this guide, you'll learn how all these qualities fit together.

The Role of Graphic Facilitator

Graphic facilitation is serving a group by writing and drawing their conversation live and large to help them do their work.

You are a facilitator. To facilitate is to make easy. You are working on behalf of the group to make their meeting easier. You take on this role to help keep the group focused and productive. You are process-focused, and know how to reflect their process and their progress through visuals.

You use graphics. You go beyond writing lists on flipcharts. You know how to use color, line and scale to make your charts visually organized and appealing. You use your thinking skills to organize the information and find patterns and make connections. You know when to write and when to draw; words and images work in tandem.

You work large. You draw and write on very large pieces of paper. Day to day work happens on letter-sized sheets of paper and flipcharts. We let bigger work happen on bigger paper. Working on a larger scale allows you not only to be seen, but to create one large, cohesive map of a conversation.

You work live. This allows people to see their conversation take shape in real time. The people in the room see what they are saying, letting them focus on the conversation, follow the progression, go back to earlier points and see the accumulation of their work.

You help the group. You work to create shared meaning for the group. I have worked with corporations, non-profits, internet start-ups, government agencies, educational institutions and more. Every one of these industries—every sector—is made up of people wanting to do good work, people who want to understand and be understood. We all want to make meaning of the work we do. We want our meetings to be meaningful and productive.

Graphic facilitation is a powerful tool to help people feel heard, to develop a shared understanding as a group and be able to see and touch their work in a way they couldn't access before.

10

Graphic facilitation is equal parts listening, thinking and drawing:

The listening is the input, the thinking is the processing and the drawing is the output. Drawing is seen as the rock star. Listening is the silent hero. And neither would mean anything without our meaning-making machine between our ears and behind our eyes.

These three skills work together equally. Throughout the book, I will not-so-gently remind you that it's not this:

Because drawing is the visible, tangible skill and because it can be the scariest and least-developed, we overemphasize it. Do not let drawing eclipse the importance of your listening and thinking skills. Yes, drawing is important. Yes, I am drawing's Number One Fan. I want you to keep it in perspective within the role of graphic facilitation. Let drawing serve you and your clients. Don't fall under its spell.

Graphic Facilitation Involves:

☐ Listening

☐ Reading the mood of the room and understanding group dynamics

☐ Responding to clients and working with facilitators

☐ Understanding process and how different methodologies help people work together

☐ Distilling wording down to its salient points

☐ Using legible penmanship

☐ Spelling

☐ Drawing fast

☐ Using color, line and iconography to make your charts dynamic and engaging

☐ Organizing the information you hear to make it more clear and easier to understand

☐ Synthesizing that information into a cohesive, resonant picture

☐ Managing your own energy and focus while doing all of the above

whew That is a lot all at once. I know. Each of us has different skills and strengths. Coming into this work, you may excel at one or two of these. You need to cultivate the weaker skills. The goal is not to be perfect in all of them, but to get stronger. Challenge yourself to develop and integrate all these skills so you can be the best graphic facilitator you can be. This is rewarding work, and this book will give you a place to navigate from.

Graphic Facilitation Terms

Graphic Facilitator
Who is mapping the meeting

The graphic facilitator listens to the group, thinks about how to organize what they hear, and maps it out using a combination of writing and drawing.

Graphic facilitators have many modes of working and tools to use. They commonly work live, drawing on large sheets of paper with markers. He or she should be well-versed in how to adapt the tool of graphic facilitation to the needs of the meeting.

Graphic facilitation is also referred to as graphic recording, scribing, visual facilitation and visual recording.

13

Facilitator
Who is running the meeting

Facilitators design the agenda of the meeting with the client and keep the meeting running smoothly. They may be internal to the client's company or external. Generally speaking, a facilitator's expertise comes in process, not content.

Facilitators can team with graphic facilitators in varying degrees, from very little to a collaborative partner in the process design.

Sometimes a client plays the facilitator role. Sometimes there is no facilitator.

Client
Who convenes the meeting

The client is bringing together the group to meet a specific objective. The client is the key person invested in the meeting being productive. Generally speaking, the client's expertise is the content of their business. They often partner with facilitators to bring the right processes and methodologies to make the event a success.

If you are an external graphic facilitator, you may be contracting with a facilitator or the client. Often, the true client is not your point of contact, but their boss. It is useful to watch the dynamics between facilitators, clients, and client bosses to adapt to who needs what.

Group, Audience, Participants
Who is in the meeting

These are the people you are mapping for. You could be working with an individual or a room of hundreds. It is their conversation or presentation that you are responsible to capture. It is vital to integrate all the voices and perspectives equally into your maps.

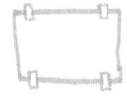

Chart, Map, Drawing
The map of the meeting

The physical map or the digital file of the map. These images are a combination of writing and drawing and ideally are organized in a way that reflects the shape and patterns in the conversation.

These charts need to be legible and engaging. They aid the process, helping the group focus on the work at hand. They also serve as a product, a snapshot of the meeting.

Ideally, graphic facilitators, facilitators and clients work together to get copies of these images distributed to all meeting attendees as soon as possible. This allows the group to move their work forward faster and more effectively.

Meeting

Any assembly of people working to meet an objective. Meetings can take on many forms and use many different kinds of methodologies and processes.

Some meetings, like annual conferences, can be primarily about presentation. A single speaker may be sharing information. Other meetings seek input from different constituencies, like a town hall meeting. Strategic planning meetings or brainstorming sessions tend to be more conversational, with everyone talking. Other meetings, like training or workshops, seek to develop skills.

Graphic facilitators should be able to adapt to different meeting formats and also know what scenarios they work best in. A professional graphic facilitator can help a client or facilitator identify where and when they will get the most value from the addition of their services.

Plenary

The parts of the meeting where the whole group is assembled together and shares the same experience.

Breakout session

Portions of the meeting when the whole group is split into smaller groups all working in parallel.

Report Out

The breakout session ends and the group reconvenes. Members from each team share what their group talked about.

Bringing Your Graphic Facilitation Skills into Other Roles

As you focus on the specific role of a graphic facilitator, its functions and its powers, you will see opportunities to apply the skills far more broadly.

While this guide focuses on using these skills to serve groups, you can apply them to your solo work. You can cultivate your listening, thinking and drawing skills to improve your note taking, learning and ability to think through your ideas.

This book describes working live and large. You can transfer these principles to working in a sketchbook or on your computer. You could use these ideas for a studio project, versus a live event.

These principles can be applied when you're working with any kind of group, whether you're internal or external. Whether you are a graphic facilitator, student, facilitator, manager, team member, teacher, coach, life-long learner or long lost drawer:

You became a **graphic facilitator**. Now your business is mapping meetings, conferences and workshops. You travel with pens and paper in hand, ready to serve your clients.

As a **student**, you used this book to help you earn a gold medal in note-taking in school. You threw out your lined paper and now you fill sketchbooks in class. You create maps of the lectures. Organizing the ideas spatially, you make new connections that you never made on lined paper. When you are assigned a paper, you draw it out first. A blank page isn't daunting because you can already visualize the shape of the whole assignment.

You used this book to strengthen your visual muscles as a **facilitator**. Now when you approach a flipchart, you're more confident and agile. You give your participants more visual tools to use themselves. You partner with graphic facilitators when the need arises and better understand how to work together to get your clients the best results.

You are a **manager** and you used this book to run better meetings. You illicit ideas from your team and you can now show them how you're listening and learning from them as you record their ideas. Your team can now see all their input together and see it from a new perspective.

You are a **team member** tackling a really complex, tangled project. You know you and your colleagues have the smarts to solve this problem. You know that sitting in meetings and talking at each other isn't cracking the code. You shared copies of this book with your teammates. Now you all convene around whiteboards, pens in hand, and map out the intricacies of the project collaboratively.

As a **teacher**, you use graphic facilitation both to organize your own lessons as well as teaching the tool to your students. Giving your students markers and blank paper alongside lined paper and computers gives them more materials for learning. You and your students create maps of the lessons, allowing everyone to tap into spatial and visual intelligences.

You are a **coach** who works one-on-one with people. You've adopted graphic facilitation as a tool to show your clients where they are, what they are saying, and where they can go.

You are a **lifelong learner** and you now bring your sketchbook to museums and lectures. Drawing helps you make meaning of your experiences. When you look back at these pages of drawings, you are brought back to that time and place. You don't lose what you've learned.

You are a **long-lost drawer**. You used to love to draw. Somewhere along the way you were told (or told yourself) you couldn't draw. This book helped you broaden your definition of drawing and you picked up your pens again. Now when you think out an idea, you see it in your head and you grab paper and write it down. You get a new perspective on it. You go farther with it.

Years later, you flip open this book. You see it's worn out and marked up. And the best thing is you don't need to read it again, because all of it is now second nature. It's now how you naturally work. You know when to use the tool of graphic facilitation.

A tiny fraction of people holding this book right now are doing so to become a graphic facilitator. There is an enormous amount of space and opportunity for graphic facilitators in our ever-more complex world. There are hundreds more opportunities for anyone and everyone to apply these principles and skills to their current work. You may wear the uniform of another vocation, but you can always put on your GF hat. Or better yet, your GF gloves.

You can use all the ways you serve groups to serve yourself. Developing your listening skills makes you more understanding, more focused, more attentive. Developing your thinking skills makes you a critical thinker, better at decision making. Developing your drawing skills gives you a tool to get your ideas out of your head and onto paper.

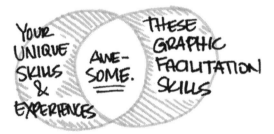

I hope you'll adopt and adapt the tools and skills in this book. Use them in new ways I have never experienced or imagined.

This is Your Guide

This field of work is wide open. There's an enormous amount of unchartered territory and open, fertile fields. Most of us are solo adventurers, uncertain of where to go. I want this book to be your guide.

There are an infinite number of places to go in this work and ways to get there. This book is not about giving you a single path to one destination. It is not a step-by-step guide. I want you to make your own way.

To that end, this book is set up with three Powers and 25 Principles. Think of the Powers as a set of lenses.

Like a microscope, each lens brings meetings into sharper focus, showing what couldn't be seen.

Like a telescope, each lens broadens our perspective and shows us the bigger picture.

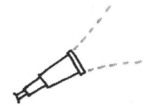

Together, these lenses create a powerful instrument that you can use.

Imagine the Principles as stars in the sky. Let them be your beacons, your reference points to navigate by. They shine above you, helping you navigate your own route. You can fix your attention on one star or gaze upon the whole night sky. Clusters of these principles fit together in constellations. These stars are constant. They are always there for reference and direction.

Every Principle gets to the Why behind What we do. Most Principles ends with a section, In Practice, which will help guide you toward developing your own How. Use these tips to make these concepts take hold through action.

Throughout this guide, I share stories from my experiences in these gray boxes.

I Am Your Guide

There is no one way to do this work. It is vital that you discover your own best way of working. If you put markers in the hands of 100 people in front of the same conversation, you'll get 100 different drawings. I want you to make your own fantastic maps. I want to be your guide.

I am hardcore about this work. I am thrilled at this opportunity to dive deep into defining why graphic facilitation is powerful and how we can do better work. I'll give you these stars to navigate by, but I won't hold your hand. I can give you these principles and the push of permission to go figure out what works for you. I hope my challenging tone is tempered with some humor along the way.

I am a practitioner, not a scholar. I can't sprinkle these pages with data, research and citations. I can give you what I know to be true from my career of doing the work.

While my writing style is conversational and you'll see my drawings and photos of me throughout this book, it is not about The Brandy Way. I believe the principles in this book are universal to the work. They will guide you to doing more effective and powerful work. How you apply and practice these principles is up to you.

Please use this guide to do your own great work. I worked to create drawings and diagrams to illustrate the Principles. While some are drawn in my style, some are more basic.

Folks attribute, or misattribute, "Good artists borrow, great artists steal" to Picasso. While we all need to start somewhere, we don't need Brandy clones. I want you to do work that is brilliantly you, that is true to your hand, experience and style.

BRANDY

BASIC

By you

I also worked hard to create a guide that encompasses all the skills in the work. These parts fit together into a whole. I designed this book to this length, size and black-and-white format to keep the price low for you. To those ends, I want you to learn from the book, and welcome you to teach from it. Please respect the intellectual property of my work and do not copy sections without my written permission. Additional copies can always be purchased at **GraphicFacilitator.com**. To share the value of the work with others, I offer the chapter **The Powers of Graphic Facilitation** (pages 35-42) as a free PDF on GraphicFacilitator.com.

End of lecture. Back to rousing call to arms.

I am confident that the listening, thinking and drawing skills you cultivate in this role will serve you and the groups you work with very well. The world will always need people who can see the big picture, who listen, who find patterns and make connections. Our world is complex and needs you to strengthen your ability to capture and organize ideas. We need more clarity. We need more shared understanding. We need more graphic facilitators in the world.

I want you to listen deeply, think critically and draw swiftly to make great work happen.

How to Succeed with This Guide

This is a book. Many things can be learned from a book. Graphic facilitation doesn't happen in the 12 inches of space between your eyes and this page. Graphic facilitation takes place live, in rooms with groups of people and giant sheets of paper. Use this book to guide your practice. The best way to understand this work is by doing it.

Mark it up. Write and draw in the book, throw it in your tool bag, add your notes from your experience. Make it a working tool for you.

Create a space. When you don't have groups to work with live, set up a studio space to practice. The best way to practice is to be standing, drawing and writing vertically and working large-scale.

This can be as simple as pounding two nails into the back of a door and hanging a pad of flipchart paper on them. Any flat wall can act as a temporary studio space. A chalk board or a dry erase board works. Living in a 570 square-foot apartment, I've got two five-foot spans of wall to work on. It works.

Don't get too fancy. Just get to it. Work large. Work vertically. Work live.

28

A flipchart hangs on my door to the right of where I hang larger paper.

Develop a practice. Refine your work and build confidence through practice. There are enormous amounts of content online to listen to: Videos, podcasts, radio, audio books. Anything you can listen to can be fodder for practice. Go to lectures and practice in work meetings. You can find more details on developing your practice with the later Principle **Practice Makes Progress.**

Find a buddy. If you are the type of person who best learns in a group and by talking things through, find people to learn with. You all can read this guide together and compare notes. Map the same talks and see how you each captured them differently. Challenge each other.

Seek other sources. While I think I'm seriously awesome, I'm not the only source for you to learn from. Look to others for information, advice and examples. Learn different perspectives. Find who you resonate on the same frequency with. We all have had teachers we've connected to and others we haven't.

Most of all, I hope you'll learn how to guide yourself in your own practice, keeping those other perspectives in perspective.

Dive in. If you have a group to work with, be brave and jump in. This is the best education you can get.

Here's a secret. Very, very few people have a point of reference to what you're doing. Graphic facilitation is brand-new to them. They won't be sitting there thinking, "Sheesh, I miss Brandy's pointy nose guys." They will be focused on their conversation and how you are capturing it. It feels like a scary proposition, but it is quite low-risk and very high-reward.

Tag it. I am thrilled to be your guide in this book, but I hope we all can learn from each other. Please use the tags in the header's upper right-hand corner to continue the conversation.

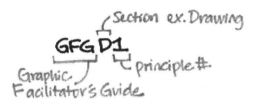

Here are all the tags:

GFGrole   The Role of Graphic Facilitator

GFGguide   Using this Guide

GFGpower   The Powers of Graphic Facilitation

GFGprinc   The Principles of Graphic Facilitation
Overview
            GFGO1   Be Seen
            GFGO2   It is Not About You
            GFGO3   Content is King
            GFGO4   Quick Like a Bunny
            GFGO5   Process Over Product
            GFGO6   Right Tools for the Job
Listening
            GFGL1   Stop & Listen
            GFGL2   Listen with Outsider Ears
            GFGL3   Not All Speakers are Created Equal
            GFGL4   Distill
Thinking

On Twitter, you can post "I rocked a colossally big piece of paper to tackle my writing project. #GFGT1."

Or you can post a photo of a chart on Flickr and add the tag GFGD2E3 because you used a limited color palette to great effect. Of course, the future will bring us new sites, apps, mind-blowing who-knows-what. You get the general idea. If we tag and reference our work this way, we can track the conversations we are having and learn from each other. We all do better work. We all win.

The Powers of Graphic Facilitation

Graphic facilitation is a powerful tool. Again, I picture the Powers like a set of lenses. They help concentrate a group inward and notice details, nuance, things previously unseen—like a microscope. Like a telescope, they focus outward to better understand the big picture and the larger context of the conversation.

 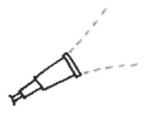

From the most basic text on a flipchart to the most elaborate murals, **the following three Powers are present every time a graphic facilitator maps a meeting**:

THE POWER OF BEING LISTENED TO

Have you experienced meeting fatigue? Been in a meeting and thought, "Uh, why am I here?" Sure, sometimes meetings are only meant to disseminate information, but often they are convened to seek input. Perhaps you have felt that your input wasn't heard, valued or acted upon.

We each listen in the meeting, but we each listen through our own politics, agenda, pressures, distractions. We retain a fraction of what we hear, most of it connected to our own responsibilities.

A graphic facilitator is the public listener, the human resource dedicated to collecting all those voices, inputs and ideas—and recording them. Whether we work internally or externally to the group, we should **Listen with Outsider Ears**. The graphic facilitator should listen to the conversation unencumbered by politics or responsibilities. Often, our lack of specific content or industry knowledge allows us to more easily see the patterns in the conversation and distill the ideas with less jargon or industry speak.

We often enter a meeting thinking about what we need to say, to speak our peace. When you express your idea, the graphic facilitator captures and writes it on the piece of paper. Once you can see that you have been heard and your input will not be lost, you can more readily listen to others. You can contribute more to the whole meeting.

THE POWER OF SHARED UNDER-STANDING

Little work is done in isolation. And individual work is often later shared. We all want our work to matter. To be understood. To be valued by others.

Our maps facilitate shared understanding. We capture all the individual voices in a conversation and integrate them into a collective image. Our maps become a record of the shared experience of the meeting, retreat, workshop or conference.

A graphic facilitator aids understanding through her or his abilities to organize the information being shared, and synthesize it into a clear whole.

These drawings are made live, so the understanding can happen immediately and be built upon. Pardon the cliché, but everyone is literally on the same page.

We assemble in groups to work on common objectives. We can accomplish more than we could as individuals. The group has its own function and identity separate from the individual identities and egos. Our maps represent the group identity and progress.

Often, groups don't come to complete consensus on all priorities or decision-making during the meeting. The shared experience is embedded in the images created, and help the group continue the work. These maps can be referenced to further build understanding and make informed decisions.

While this book concentrates on shared, group experiences, the ideas can also be used one-on-one, to share your thinking with another person in an organized image as a communication tool. Two people can co-create a map to think through their ideas together. You can use these principles to clarify your own learning and thinking, working alone.

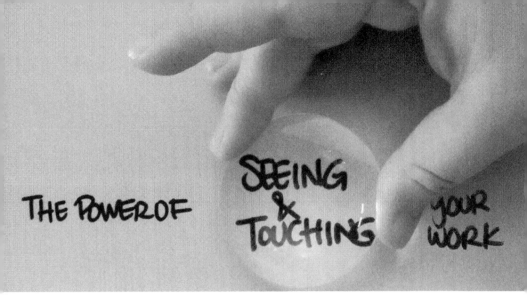

THE POWER OF SEEING & TOUCHING YOUR WORK

Seeing is making the work visible, transparent. Touching is making the work tangible, concrete.

Transparency and tangibility are important both at the meeting and after the meeting.

In the meeting, everyone watches their conversation take shape. Everyone can see the work made tangible on the map. Everyone can find clarity within the complexity through a well-organized drawing.

The process of the group is recorded in the maps. The group can track their progress during the meeting and can reflect on it afterwards.

Over the course of the meeting, the number of drawings accumulates. On a day that is filled with plenary discussion, I can fill four to five pieces of paper, roughly four feet tall and six feet long. That is over 100 square feet of output per day. It is difficult to doubt the productivity of a meeting when you see the walls covered in the work.

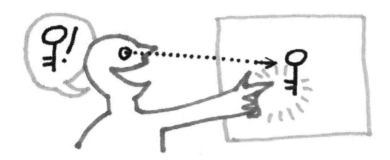

Our work and ideas can be tied up in conflict and internal politics, or simple miscommunication. The map acts as a mediator. It is an object that everyone can focus on outside of themselves and away from each other. You may see Jack as the root of the problem going into the meeting. Once the problem gets written up on the map, you can see the problem from a new perspective, and hopefully distanced enough from Jack to make it less emotionally charged and more easily solved.

We make time, we shuffle schedules and sometimes we travel far and wide for a Very Important Conversation. These VIC's occur and then you head back to your day-to-day work. What do you remember of that meeting? How important does it feel?

If your VIC had a GF, you have the images they create to use as an artifact. Your team can use the maps as a reference and as a snapshot of where you were on that date. You are all better-equipped to build on the momentum of the meeting and take your work farther, faster.

Lastly, the maps are large, colorful and engaging. They are unlike anything that typically lives in our workplace. These drawings are refreshing and help everyone see their meeting in a new, colorful light.

At the end of a strategic planning session with a hundred hospital administrators, a woman stood and waved toward the walls covered in their maps: "I am so thankful for the color on the walls and seeing our work look so bright and vibrant. It makes me feel like a kid again and I didn't realize how much I missed it. I'm going to take some of this color back to the hospital with me."

She was quite emotional when she shared this, and it certainly struck my heart. Beauty does feed us.

These Powers are Universal

I have worked across industries and sectors, with companies tiny, enormous, brand-new and tried-and-true. My experience tells me graphic facilitation works for anyone who values being listened to, teams who want to understand each other—those who want to see their work made transparent and tangible.

Yes, there are individual people who aren't receptive to it. If that person is the decision-maker on hiring you, you won't get in the door. There are endless other doors with decision-makers ready to welcome you and your skills.

I rankle when I hear a colleague say, "Only non-profits get what we do" or "Government agencies don't understand our work." Every company or organization is made up of people who want to be understood and to make meaning of their work. I am more likely to fault my colleague for not being able to describe their role and its value clearly. It is difficult to put into words, and the best way to really understand the value of graphic facilitation is to experience it. I have seen success from my colleagues in every industry and sector.

Yes, you should get to know each client's specific needs and their organization's culture and norms. Be adaptable to how a school board may need something different from you than a Fortune 500 leadership team. From my experience, we are far more alike than different. Enjoy the universalities and be receptive and flexible to work with the differences.

Focus These Powers on Your Process

While I believe every client or participant can appreciate graphic facilitation, not every event or process is the right fit. Though many, many are. This book is process-agnostic. We could fill a bookcase designing for each and every methodology in an Encyclopedia of Graphically Facilitated Processes. And those volumes still wouldn't be able to describe each unique situation. In these 298 pages, I can't tell you how to specifically map a World Café or how to capture an Open Space event.

I believe that by remembering these Powers and guiding yourself with the following Principles, you will learn where and when you can best serve your clients.

The Principles of Graphic Facilitation

As a guide, this book is not turn-by-turn driving directions or a detailed roadmap. Instead, I've created a star map of principles from which to navigate. While you work, you can focus of one principle, consider a constellation or view the whole sky. These principles fall into five areas:

Overview
Your closest, brightest six stars. They apply to the work as a whole, not a specific skill.

Listening
Four stars focus on the input you gather as you listen and observe a group.

Thinking
Six stars are about how you process what you hear, how you organize the ideas into clear, cohesive maps.

Drawing
A single star and a star cluster guide the output of writing and drawing. The final star addresses how thinking and drawing work together with synthesis.

Practicing
Three stars guide refining and improving your work over time.

In the Room
Three stars address what happens live in the room and how you relate to your clients.

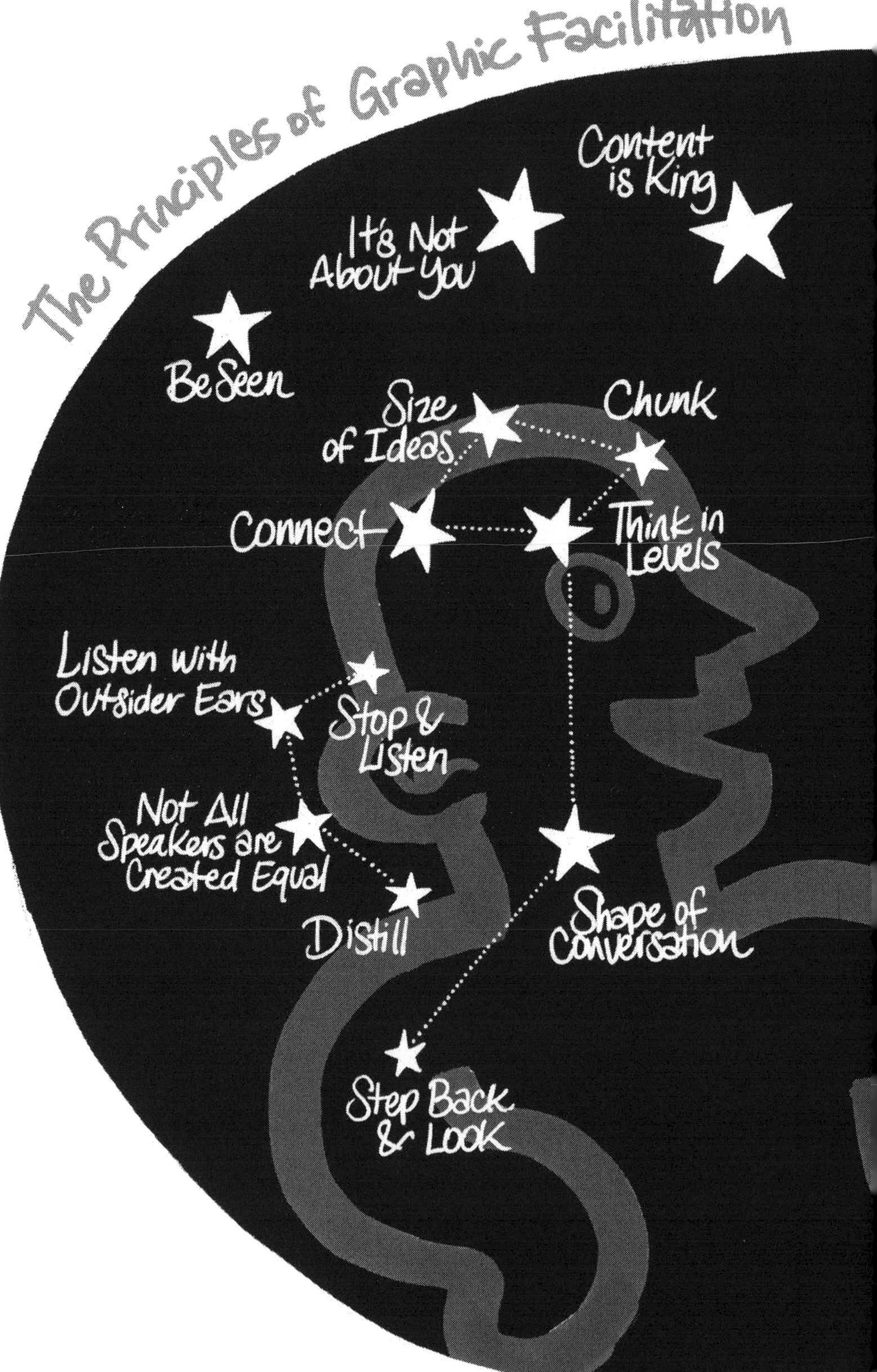

The Principles of Graphic Facilitation

Content is King

It's Not About You

Be Seen

Size of Ideas

Chunk

Connect

Think in Levels

Listen with Outsider Ears

Stop & Listen

Not All Speakers are Created Equal

Distill

Shape of Conversation

Step Back & Look

by Brandy Agerbeck

Quick Like a Bunny

Process Over Product

the Essential Eight

Right Tools for the Job

Every Mark has Meaning

Putting It Together

Practice Makes Progress

Challenge Yourself

Build Your Visual Vocabulary

Partner Up

Give them the Markers

Your Presence is Powerful

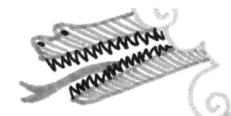

Here Be Dragons

You are striking out into the unknown. You are creating your own map. I know this may be scary. Only by stepping into the work—and standing in front of people—will you truly learn the work. You will find your own way.

Although human beings have been drawing on cave walls since forever, and the field of graphic recording and facilitation began in the 1970s, this work is still brand-new to most people. We live on the edges of the map. There are a lot of unknowns—and miles of new territory to discover for yourself.

The more you explore, the more you can anticipate and adapt to new terrain. I know the Principles will keep you on a productive path.

Take the first step. Enjoy the adventure.

Be Seen

Let's start with the obvious. You need to be seen. You've got to put the graphic into graphic facilitation.

Notice that the powers of graphic facilitation are about what happens live in the room. It is a process. To be most effective, the group needs to see you work in real-time to see their own conversation take shape.

If you are brand-new to the work, you may hear your heart thumping or your knees knocking at the prospect of standing in front of the room.

It is entirely your choice when it come to how you work. There are people who work at the sides of the room, at the back of the room, even small-scale at desks, or in sketchbooks in their laps. They are still producing useful images, but they are giving up a fantastic opportunity—the opportunity to let the group see the image being created. To see their voices made visible. To be facilitated by the graphics.

Being seen is about placement, scale, legibility. Be at the right spot in the room where the most people can see you. Use markers that make lines and colors which can be seen from a distance. Write large and legibly. Step out of the way of your work, so people can see it.

You can't know or control your audience's eyesight; not everyone will see you 20/20. Control the factors you can control.

Another variable is group size. When working with a dozen people, it is easy for everyone to see you. They all can watch you write and draw and interact with the map. In a ballroom filled with 1,000 people, you'd be visible to one or two tables closest to you.

You won't have the same impact on those 1,000 conference attendees as you have on those 12 people in a strategic planning session. Adapt your circumstances to have the most impact possible. For example, in large events, a videographer can record you and play your work on large screens. Or you can set up your finished charts in a common area to be seen during breaks or meals.

In Practice

Get front and center. Talk to the facilitator, client or meeting planner about the room and determine where you can best be seen. If you are mapping an event for hundreds of people, talk to the producers about being well-lit, being on a stage, and being video-recorded.

Be well-lit. Many of our meetings and conferences take place in cave-like rooms without windows, rooms better suited for growing mushrooms than people thinking clearly. And lighting often doesn't extend to the edges of the ceilings. Place yourself in the best light or arrange lights to highlight your work.

Work large. We will talk more about what to draw with and what to draw on in **Right Tools for the Job**. Most graphic facilitators use rolls of paper that are four feet tall. We then cut our paper to fit the space, or pre-cut it to six- or eight-foot lengths. Working larger than flipchart-sized paper allows us to capture longer conversations and also map all the ideas into one large image.

Use tools with best visibility. Work with markers that make lines and ink colors which can be seen at a distance. Only use light colors for highlights or shading.

Make your work clear and legible. Work on your penmanship. Develop a drawing style that is easy to read. Align the scale of your writing and drawing to the scale of the paper, the audience size, the room set-up.

Don't get in your own way. Practice writing with your arm extended, to avoid blocking your own work. Step out of the way when you're listening.

I was mapping an internal strategy meeting of about two dozen people. During a break, I walked by a trio of people huddled around a flipchart. They were drawing text and very rough diagrams in yellow marker. They wrote toward the top of the page, in the shadow of the previous sheet folded over. I winced at the illegibility of their work, fearing it wouldn't be seen by the whole group when they shared it. I offered them a darker marker. One person politely declined, "Oh no, we're whispering."

It's Not About You

You are playing a vital role in these meetings. It is not about you.

You are bringing very important skills into that space. It is not about you.

You are doing something many people have never seen. It is novel and exciting. You will get a lot of praise. It is not about you.

You may get paid handsomely to do this very intense, highly skilled work. It is not about you.

It is about the people in the room. It is about their conversation. It is about their work.

You are there to serve them.

This is not to say that you're less than these people, the conversation or the work. Graphic facilitation is not a subordinate role. It is to say that you are there to facilitate. It's about the process and progress the group makes. It is not about you. It's about your facilitating their work.

Be Seen. As graphic facilitators we stand at the front of the room. We work on giant sheets of paper. All eyes are on us. These things signal a performance. That placement is usually reserved for the CEO, speaker or facilitator. We tend to think of the person at the front of the room as commanding our attention.

You *do* want their focus, the attention, to be seen. You want all those things because your work in this role helps the group do better work. You use your skills to create a drawing, a map that facilitates their meeting.

It is about the group. It is about the work.

The yin to **It's Not About You**'s yang is: **It's About the Group**. You are working for the group. And they will appreciate you for it. The group is with you, not against you. They will be quick to ignore a spelling mistake and if you miss a point, they will help you catch it. Because you are there to help them, people are very happy to help you.

In Practice

Be introduced. You should always, always be introduced at the beginning of a meeting. Many will be curious and perhaps agitated by seeing someone standing at a giant piece of paper. Your role is new and unfamiliar. Highlight how you are there to serve them and invite them to work with you and your images.

I always go for a very brief introduction, nothing more than "I'm Brandy and I'm a graphic facilitator. I'm here to map your conversation today. Once I get going it'll make perfect sense. You will get copies of the images after the meeting."

Occasionally, I work a big, fancy conference that wants a more formal bio. As I listen to "internationally published, umpteen years, etc." I feel that I will prove my worth and my experience as soon as I uncap my maker and get going. It's not about me and what I've accomplished. It is about what I can help the group accomplish.

Serve. Remember that you are there in service. Always ask yourself, "How can I help this group?"

Don't distract. Be seen, but don't pull focus away from the conversation. Watch your body language. Stand still; don't fidget or pace. We'll look at this in detail in the Principle **Your Presence is Powerful** on page 283.

Accept compliments within context. Be gracious and focus on the work. Participants will comment on your drawing, or penmanship, or be generally effusive and excited. It is very rewarding. A large factor in their positive feelings is that you're helping them do better work. Don't get caught up in the praise and don't dismiss your skills either. I personally opt for a response that puts the focus back on the work, such as, "Thank you. I'm so glad you're finding my work useful."

Content is King

After very abruptly being told **It's Not About You**, it is about the *content*. What is content? It is what happens in the meeting. It is the information shared, conversation spoken, ideas generated, priorities set, decisions made or meeting objectives met.

Think of a meeting like a container. That meeting is in a certain space, takes place for a set amount of time, with the people present and the conversation they share. Content is what is held by that container of a meeting. **Content is King**. Your maps should reflect the content of the meeting.

As you work as a graphic facilitator, always remember the content of the meeting, the work being done. Think about how your drawings help that work go farther, faster and be better.

You start with a giant blank sheet of paper. How do you know you've reflected the content? Here are some factors:

Everyone feels their input and time is valued.

From emphasizing one person's input over another's.

To showing everyone's input together and representing the connections and patterns.

From attributing content to a specific speaker.

To not attributing an idea to a specific person, because it is about the idea, not who said it.

Understanding through shared ideas and information.

From getting caught up in your drawing, and missing the conversation.

To keeping drawing in equal proportion to your listening and thinking, so you never distract yourself with drawing.

From lists of unsorted ideas.

To similar ideas grouped, showing relationships between ideas.

The map has the integrity of what happened within the timeframe of the meeting.

From adding input or images to the chart after the conversation or meeting is over.

To making your map live during the meeting. You stop drawing when they stop talking. Things aren't added afterwards.

Priorities are set and decisions made.

From clouds of undifferentiated ideas.

To decisions and priorities being clearly shown, using highlighting, boxes or creating separate summary lists.

In Practice

Talk to the client. In a prep call, you can learn about the meeting objectives, ask about the company culture and run through the meeting agenda. Learn what the shape of the meeting's container may be and what content it may contain.

I worked with a manufacturing company that was kicking off a company culture initiative. In the prep conversation with the facilitator, she

> explained that the organization is very comfortable with talking about product, but uncomfortable with talking about people.
>
> I asked, "So if the speakers are lapsing into familiar product talk, do I have permission to not draw it?"
>
> "Oh, yes!" She replied. "Please."

Prepare. As explained in the Powers chapter, people and organizations are more alike than dissimilar. Surprisingly little content is specific to the company's products, services or industry. That being said, you can familiarize yourself with their specifics. If you are about to work with a trucking company, you may practice drawing trucks. Feel free to do this if it makes you feel more prepared and confident. Then be open to the content in the meeting. You may never need to draw a truck.

Listen, observe, respond, adapt. Responsiveness and adaptability will serve you better than preparation. Agendas change. If they do, you must adapt to the new content and let go of your preparation. Keep your ears, eyes and mind open.

I mapped a summit of 300 people discussing community initiatives in a town hall format.

I was floored that over two days, 10 people came up to me *live*, while I was drawing, to tell me their personal thoughts on the subject. They felt I had power, because I held the pen.

The true power is in voicing their input with the whole group. Then I capture it. It wouldn't facilitate the group to add comments that hadn't been shared with everyone.

I'm so laser-focused while I work. These interruptions fluster me. I probably shoot daggers from my eyes. I try to politely say, "If you say it in the meeting, I'll get it on the map."

Quick like a Bunny

Here are two bunnies:

This one took
10 seconds to draw.

This one took
10 minutes to draw.

There are occasions to draw a 10-minute bunny.
Graphic facilitation is not the time.

When someone says "rabbit," I want you to make a
quick drawing of a rabbit that captures the idea of a
rabbit. That quick drawing is now on paper. It is

tangible. And now you are free to keep listening to the next idea within the ongoing conversation.

If you start drawing the 10-minute bunny, you'll miss nine minutes and fifty seconds of the conversation. You could wow a few people in the audience with your phenomenal bunny drawing prowess. Others in the room will notice you missed the mark. And you would have.

Be **Quick Like a Bunny.**

You are working live. There is no giant pause button you can push to stop the conversation. The speed with which you work is critical.

When I teach workshops, we all map the same recorded video at the same time. Afterward, I ask, "So, how did that go?"

Number one response: *"It was so fast."*

It is.

Because **Content is King**, it is your responsibility to keep up with the group, not for the group to slow down to you.

This isn't only about drawing pictures, though this is where I see people slow down the most. You could write impeccably, but very slowly. You could sketch in pencil first, delaying any visible marks until you draw those sketches in ink. You could be so enamored with shading in your chart with pastels that you lose yourself.

In Practice

Do speed drills. Actively practice with speed in mind. Work on writing as fast and as legibly as possible. Develop iconography that is quick to draw.

Don't fall in love with the drawing. Drawing is tons of fun. I adore it. In the context of graphic facilitation it is simply the output. And the input, listening to the conversation, will keep coming. You may adore drawing

They are very slow. **Content is King**. You aren't serving the king with 3-D block letters.

Write the beginning of words. Someone says, "Our team's top priorities are quality product, impeccable customer service and industry leadership." You can first write:

- qual
- cust
- indust   You can then fill in the rest.

Draw in stages. You can get a quick outline drawn, then listen for the next point. When there is a lull in conversation, go back and add details, add shading.

Make notes. Keep sticky notes handy to quickly scribble down points and then write them in later.

Ask for help. The group wants you to succeed. They quickly understand how you are helping them and they want to help you. Ask for assistance in a way that keeps the meeting flowing. You could get flustered and say "Wait! Slow down!" It is very disruptive. Instead, keep your calm and ask for help filling in the spots you missed.

I am lightning-fast, but occasionally several things will come up in rapid succession. One of my best clients is great at keeping an eye on me. She's kind enough to say, "Let's give Brandy a minute." I appreciate that she looks out for me *and* it completely stalls the conversation and people fall dead silent.

I prefer to ask, "I know I missed a point, can someone help?" People are happy to help, and this way of asking for help keeps the report out flowing.

Hit the emergency pause button. If you are really drowning, ask everyone to put each of their ideas on a sticky note. Either the participants or a facilitator can hand them to you. You can arrange each one in the right places and then write them on the chart. This method works when the group is generating a list, and would not work in a conversation.

A note on notes: Jotting notes and sketching things in are a way to get something down fast. They also add another step to your process. Practice getting the content captured on the first round first. Don't lean too hard on these crutches that add another step.

Process Over Product

We stand in front of people and make giant drawings. Since we are creating a thing, it's easy to get caught up in the thing. We need to focus on the creating part. The **ing-ing**.

In our meet**ing**s, we are talk**ing**, learn**ing**, shar**ing**, debat**ing**, prioritiz**ing**, decid**ing**. As a graphic facilitator, you are mapping those **–ings**, the process. Yes, it does result in a useful product. Favor process over product.

While not scientific, I think of graphic facilitation as 80% Process and 20% Product. I feel my clients hire me to facilitate through visuals, not so they can buy the drawings I create.

We can easily get overly occupied with the product. There are many reasons:

Listening is intangible. Thinking is intangible. Drawing is tangible. The tangible object is easier to focus on and control. It is the skill we can see.

The drawing means nothing without the listening and thinking behind it. Favor substance over style. Take an ugly, content-rich map over a pretty, empty one any day.

We can't control the meeting. Often we witness messy conversations, tensions or conflict. Making a tidy image makes us feel better. We can control the drawing.

Yes, we do strive to bring clarity to the conversations. Some maps are messy because the conversations are. Approach the process where it is, be it messy or tense.

We equate drawing with art—Art with a capital A. This association carries a lot of pressure and baggage regarding who can be an artist, who can draw, and what a Drawing is.

Think of these maps as working documents, not finished works of art.

We may feel like we are being hired for the drawings, versus the facilitation. We want our clients to be satisfied with the work product, so we may make it too packaged and finished.

Trust your ability to reflect the process. Only work while the conversation is happening to avoid busying yourself with post-work and details that don't matter.

Our clients are excited by the graphic facilitation and want to get the most value out of our work and the fees they paid us. They may elevate the physical product to a level that hinders the process.

Set expectations with your client and help them understand the value of the process. Show a variety of processes in your portfolio. Encourage them to be good stewards of the images.

The content you capture is always more important that the style or flashiness of how you capture it.

How Finished is a Drawing?

Consider these three drawing approaches to one idea:

The drawing on the left may feel too sloppy. The drawing on the right may feel too set. Like Goldilocks, the center image may be just right. It captures the idea clearly without being either so loose it doesn't feel valid, or so polished that it feels closed or rigid.

Yes, if the group has agreed on a conclusion, it may warrant an ornate frame to set it on your drawing. Ascertain how finished your drawing should or shouldn't be for the work being done.

These very detailed or refined drawings are visual cues that the idea is complete, the conversation is over. Often, the meetings we map are one part of a larger process.

The images in this guide presented a challenge. You are holding a finished product, a book. You expect a level of refinement in a printed document. I am representing a process within the book. I want the drawings to be fast and look like the images I create live. I felt the process was more important than the product, so I kept the images fast and direct. They were drawn on index cards and scanned in. I made them grayscale and popped them in the document. Very few got any kind of tweaking or modification digitally.

In Practice

Deliver the drawings. Keep the meeting's momentum by getting the images out to everyone as soon as possible. Participants can use those images as artifacts of the meeting, as a step in their process.

Don't get precious. Focus your energy on the process, not the product. It is important to label your work with your name and the date. It is not important that you splash your signature on it, like a painting canvas. Don't spend your whole break filling in shading or adding details to your map. You'll be unprepared for the next part of the group's process.

You may see all these details as your professionalism. By all means do not be sloppy in your work, but if you are too refined or precious in your work, you could be overemphasizing your product over the group's process.

Understand the baggage of Art Speak. We all come into this work from different areas. The visual, artistic, drawing part means different things to different people. For some, it opens them up to an artistic side of themselves they want to embrace. For someone like me from a fine art background, I want to shed the associations with fine art because it's about serving the group, not my own self-expression.

You can describe you and your work any way you like. Understand that words like "art" and "artist" are words that tend to separate people instead of bringing them together. People have a lot of emotional baggage about what is and isn't art and who can and can't be an artist.

Encourage best use of the images. Give the physical drawings to the people responsible for the follow-up work. Invite the group to hang the charts in a shared space. If a team is virtual, make sure they all get digital images of the charts to work from. You and your clients need to agree on what you deliver. Just keep in mind what the best product is to help your client build on the momentum of the work they accomplished in the meeting.

A community college was using their in-service day to do strategic planning with the faculty and staff. Fifty of us worked in an amphitheater classroom. I papered the front chalk boards, so I could draw permanent drawings.

Mid-meeting, the group made an agenda change. I had started a drawing on topic A. They decided they needed to switch gears, talk extensively about Topic B, then get back to Topic A as it connected to Topic C.

The best solution was to physically cut apart Topic A and B. This gave us more room to map B on the sheet of paper underneath. And I taped Topic A on to a new sheet for upcoming Topic C.

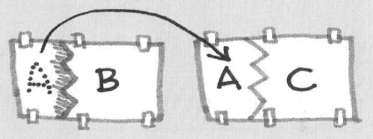

I did this with 100 eyes on me, and it wasn't swift or pretty. And I now had drawings with rough edges and pieces taped together. **But it was exactly what the group needed to get their work done.**

As we moved the chart, a participant exclaimed, "The original cut and paste!"

Right Tools for the Job

Your tools are dependent on the situation. You need the right tools for the job. You may have different tools for each job. You also have different access to different tools depending on where you live and your budget. Because tools are a personal preference and depend on your project and your access, here are criteria on how you can choose your best tools. They break down into two categories: What you draw on and what you draw with.

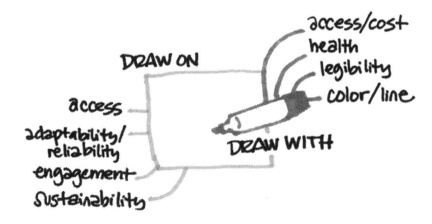

DRAW ON

access/cost
health
legibility
color/line

access
adaptability/
  reliability
engagement
sustainability

DRAW WITH

Draw On

You can do this work with any kind of surface where you can be seen. Your drawings can be temporary (white board, chalk board, smart board) or permanent (flipcharts, paper, sticky notes, foam core).

Criteria for What to Draw On:

Accessibility

You need something to draw on wherever and whenever a project arises. The surface you work on needs to be accessible, both in source and cost. Portability is also key if you are working on a client site; you can travel with all your materials or ship them ahead of time. For instance, I always travel with a new roll of paper that is four feet tall and 75 feet long. I bring it on trains, planes and automobiles. It's not tons of fun to schlep with me, but I always know it's there.

Adaptability and Reliability

Your materials must adapt to different client needs. If an agenda changes, can you easily change your materials to fit the circumstances? Your ability to work with your client's site and logistics is a strength; making your client adapt to your specifications in a liability.

I don't pre-cut my roll of paper and for this reason, I can adapt to the space and the agenda.

Engaging and Participatory

Your materials are meaningless if you're not helping the group make meaning. Is the group watching you? Are they commenting? Can you share your materials with the group to invite everyone to contribute to the big picture? The more engaging and participatory your materials, the more impact you have and the more value you create for your clients.

Sustainability

A fan of Mother Earth, I want your materials to be kind to the environment. Paper can be recycled; foamcore cannot (though I've heard murmurs of biodegradable foamcore). Consider the lifespan of your materials, how they are created and what happens to them when you're done.

Digital vs. Physical

I am very pro-technology. But I still prefer paper and pens over other possibilities. There's a directness and presence to giant sheets of paper that cannot be beat. There is a power to touching your work physically. The finished drawings are large and tangible and can be moved around, marked up and recycled when they aren't serving the group anymore.

More and more people are doing digital graphic facilitation. The tools are getting more reliable and accessible. We can still contribute our listening, thinking and drawing skills to the group through digital tools.

One word of warning: We look at screens day and night. Consider how we tune in and tune out the screens around us.

It has become quite a novelty to sit around a table together **without** screens, talking directly to each other. It's a real treat to give yourself time away from technology with a sheet of paper and some pens. It is hard to tune out a 4-foot x 8-foot piece of paper being drawn on *live*.

Experiment with both and observe how your audiences respond to the formats. The more accessible, adaptable, reliable, engaging, participatory and sustainable your materials, the better.

A technology company asked me to draw on an electronic smart board for their meeting. Aside from the markers being slightly different, my process should be exactly the same. I agreed *and* I packed my paper and markers.

Turns out we couldn't get the smart board to calibrate. I was happy to have my backup materials. Sure, paper is less flashy, but it is so reliable.

Draw With

Criteria for What to Draw With:

Accessibility and Cost

How easy is it for you to get your hands on the markers? How expensive are they? How long do they last? Are they disposable or refillable? If some jerkface steals your markers (it has happened to me), how hard are they to replace?

I opt for a marker that is from only one source, but they fit the bill perfectly and are refillable. One colleague chose a very popular brand of commercial markers. He can buy them anywhere. They are cheap; he bills the client for them. And the client keeps them when he's done. Another colleague leaves her markers and extra paper behind to empower the group to continue the work.

Health

Are your markers non-toxic, water-based, or alcohol-based? How will the inks and fumes affect you?

I'm especially passionate about this factor. In four years studying printmaking in college, I felt the physical damage from exposure to the acids, inks, solvents and aerosols. Not everyone is a canary in a coal mine, but I want all of you beautiful creatures to be well for the long term. Be safe. You are holding those markers close to your face as you stand and draw. Your brain lives behind that face, your lungs below. Take care of yourself.

Color and Line

Do you have the range of colors you need? Do you have a combination of dark colors for content and light colors for connecting and highlighting? Does the marker give you the kind of line you want? Markers generally fall into three types: chisel, bullet and brush. We will go into more detail on page 193 about line quality.

Legibility

Test your markers. Write out an alphabet. Try different thicknesses of line from your pen. Repeat this with each color. Now step back and look. Looking from a participant's distance, is your work legible? From across the room?

 Enjoy testing markers. Be aware of what they can do *for you* and *to you*.

In Practice

Test and compare. Get your hands on different tools. See how they work for you. Decide which best fits your process and style.

Use the tools. Experiment and see what options your chosen tools give you. Feel confident in your materials.

Have choices. Consider different tools to meet different project needs.

Follow the campsite rule. Always leave the client site in the same state you found it. Never leave ink stains on the walls. Use low-tack tape to leave wall paint intact. Clean up after yourself.

I began this work in an environment where we used dry erase markers on white board. The fast-paced environment taught me to draw very fast. (Some may say Quick Like a Bunny.) The surface of the dry erase boards made them very difficult to photograph with the quality of digital cameras at the time. We had to redraw each of our maps. I appreciated that the dry erase boards forced me to focus on line. Have you ever tried to fill in a solid shape with one? Sisyphean. I did not appreciate the fumes or how quickly they dried out.

When I struck out on my own, my tools of choice were four-foot rolls of paper and Mr. Sketch markers. Mr. Sketch markers are fairly easy to find, non-toxic, with really rich colors. At the time they had a perfect chisel tip. I used them for a decade.

The only drawback was that I went through a lot of

them. I pined for a more sustainable option. A colleague introduced me to Neuland markers. They had all of Mr. Sketch's good qualities and could be refilled. Now I didn't need to throw away and replace my tools. And as a bonus, they have the BigOne, which made a line twice the thickness of a Mr. Sketch. Previously, I would create thicker lines in my work by doubling or tripling the Mr. Sketch lines.

I am now devoted to Neulands. I am proud as punch to have my work on the 2011/2012 catalog cover.

Risking sounding like a sales pitch, I share how my tools have changed over time, and answer the number one most-asked question from colleagues.

Do your due diligence and see what markers work best for you.

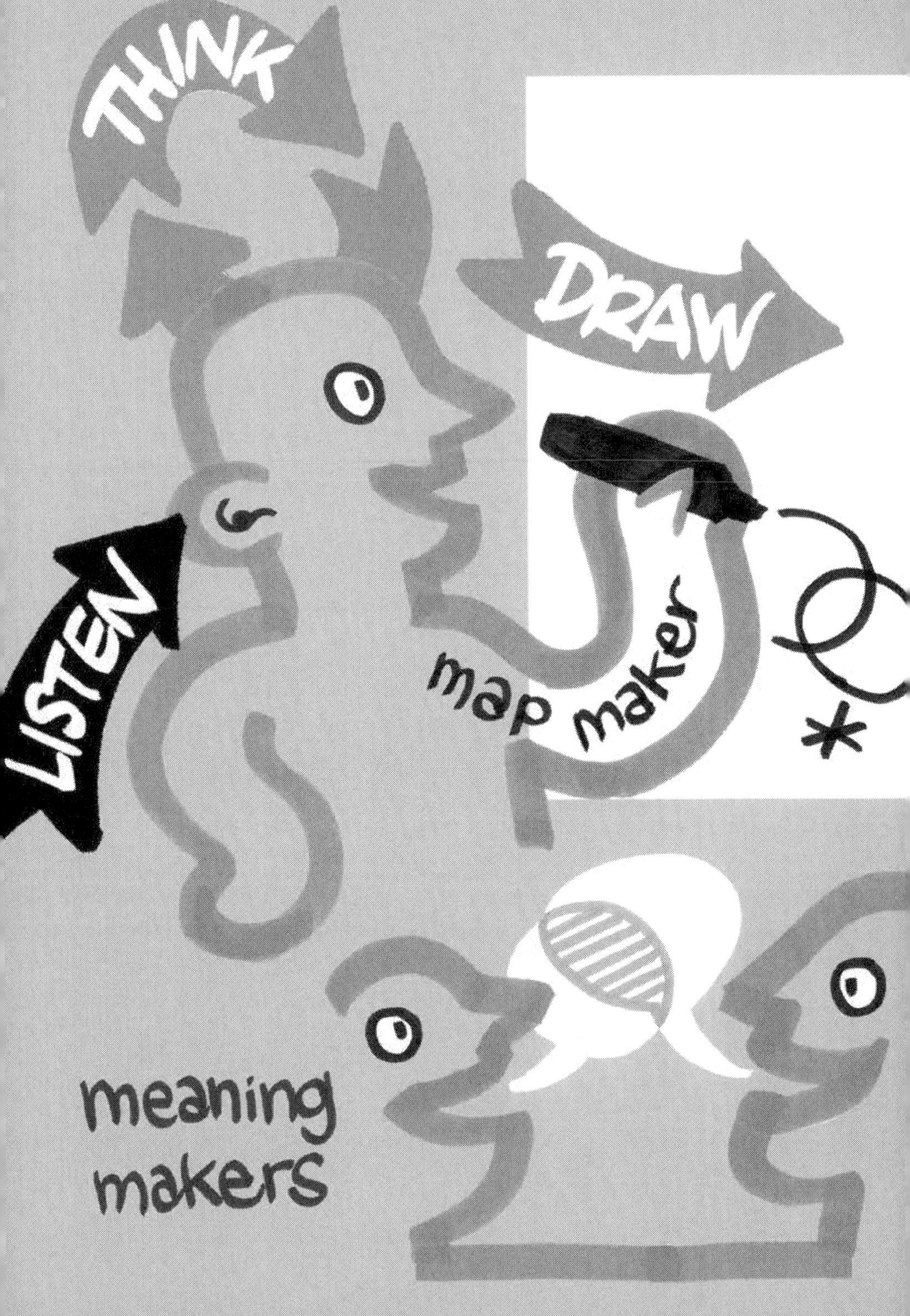
THINK
DRAW
LISTEN
map maker
meaning makers

LISTENING

Stop & Listen

We work intensely to make these live charts. Many folks feel the need to be mapping non-stop. You can stop and listen. You should stop and listen. This helps you pace yourself and gives you time to think.

Different types of meetings, using different processes, have different paces. If a group is brainstorming a list of ideas or ten teams are reporting out after a breakout session, you'll be writing and drawing nonstop. If someone is telling a story, you could be paused listening for their conclusion. You can stop and listen more easily in some meetings than others.

Stopping to listen also means facing the group so you can watch as you listen. Seeing the group's response to a comment, story or idea is a very useful clue to how to map it. For instance, The Boss may make a Big Declarative Statement.

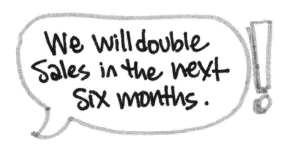

She is the boss. It sounds important. If you only listen to her, it may feel natural to write that declarative statement like this:

Now imagine that The Boss makes this statement and you watch for the group's reaction. If you see a lot of alert expressions of agreement and nodding heads, the group agrees with The Boss. The big, bold, centered image reflects both the statement and its response.

Imagine instead you see the group expressing skepticism, doubt and confusion. There isn't agreement between the speaker and the group. It doesn't mean that the speaker is wrong, it just means the collective is not with her yet. Your big, bold, centered image wouldn't fit. You could draw something like this:

This captures The Boss's statement while also expressing the doubt and leaving room for the group to discuss the topic and reach agreement.

Once they do they agree, you can recapture that key message in large letters that reinforces the shared understanding of the group.

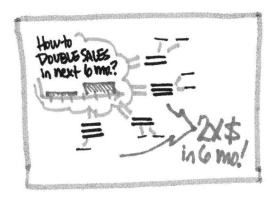

In Practice

Be still. Listen quietly and calmly. Face the group. Watch along with your listening. Watch the speaker alongside the group's response.

Get to know pacing. Over time, notice the pace of different types of meetings, and sections within a meeting. Learn how the pace of a lightning-fast brainstorming round or a report out will keep your fingers flying, whereas a keynote or an in-depth conversation will have ebbs and flows.

Keep calm and draw on. If you're brand-new to the work, you have permission to write and draw more rather than less. It can be easier to stay in capture mode and ride it out when you're uncertain. New practitioners can go into paralysis when they stop drawing. Once your beginner's anxiety wears off, know that it's okay to be quiet, attentive and not drawing while waiting for the next point.

When you find yourself distracted, don't focus on it. Gently notice it and begin listening again.

Watching a panel discussion. The left of the chart is the introduction the moderator made, sharing the context of the discussion. I stand quietly and attentively as the discussion gets underway.

An important first step in listening is being able to hear.

I had an event with a consulting company that had built their innovation center in a concrete room, filled with metal furniture and no windows. With little wood or fabric to absorb sound, all sounds bounced around the space like a ping pong ball. I had a hard time concentrating on the conversation because the sound quality was so poor.

The head honcho in this group was a man who liked to stand and listen. He paced and fidgeted, jingling the coins in his pocket.

I also like to stand and move, and being tactile, I love to have something for my hands to do as I listen. But this was a case of a noisy tic in an acoustically bad room.

I approached the man and whispered, "I'm having a hard time filtering out your coin jingling." He was apologetic and stopped. Temporarily. He started up again. He wasn't consciously doing it.

Know that it is perfectly acceptable to do whatever you can to make it easier for you to hear what's going on. Participants will quickly realize you aren't trying to reprimand them, you're just trying to do your best work.

This most often happens when multiple people are talking at once, or someone is having a side conversation. The side talkers may shoot you a miffed glance if you shush them, but more people will understand you are straining to hear.

If you have control of the space, choose rooms that aren't large and echo-y and bigger than the group needs. Soft furnishings like upholstered furniture and carpet help absorb sound well. Having clay or pipe cleaners around to fiddle with is fantastic for tactile thinkers, and they don't make additional noise.

Listen with Outsider Ears

A vital aspect of our role is that we are outside of the group, serving the group. We can see the group as a whole and are unencumbered by politics. This is golden.

We listen with outsider ears. We observe and note the dynamics of the meeting. We listen equally to all who speak, without weighing a person's idea against their position. While we may notice the politics in a group, we should not side with any one faction.

At the time of this writing, the vast majority of graphic facilitators are independent contractors rather than internal resources. Even those who are internal tend to work across departments. Over time, as this role becomes more widely known, this will change. Individuals will develop these skills to serve from within their organizations.

It is critical that you keep listening with outsider ears.

What does this mean? You very well know who the boss is or who the leaders are in the room. Do not map their inputs as more important than others. You may have your own values and issues you hold dear. For instance, you may love the environment. If you hear a client talk about sustainability, map it in proportion to the conversation, not larger than it should be because you are biased toward it. You may personally disagree with a strategy suggested. You need to suspend judgment and represent how the strategy was discussed, not what you think it should be.

It is important to differentiate: All speakers and voices are equal, although not all ideas are the same scale. You bring value to the meeting by listening to everyone and everything and helping to organize the ideas. You group ideas, link them and use scale to pull out bigger ideas and themes. Use smaller scale for supporting ideas and details. We'll go into more depth on this topic in **Think in Levels** on page 139, but here's an overview:

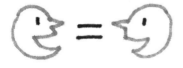 All speakers and voices within a meeting are equal. Everyone should feel valued and comfortable to speak up.

As a graphic facilitator, your role is to capture everything that happens in the meeting. Each participant should feel recognized by what you map, and that it is an accurate reflection of what is happening.

All comments and ideas should be captured. Not all comments are on the same scale within a meeting. The map should reflect the scale of both big ideas and themes alongside smaller points and details.

It is useful to separate the person from their idea. While each person has the same weight in the room, not every idea has the same weight on the map.

If the Boss does state The Big Idea, it should be drawn as The Big Idea. Listening with outsider ears means you don't identify the boss and then map each of his or her comments as if it is automatically The Big Idea.

Every person was invited to the meeting to give their input. Everyone should be heard.

A very common question you will be asked is, "How much do you know beforehand?" Or "what do you know about our industry?"

Our ignorance of a specific client's culture or industry is a distinct advantage. We aren't living with their jargon. We aren't embroiled in the politics. What you lack in industry knowledge, you make up for in adaptability, perceptivity, listening skills and objectivity.

In Practice

Divest yourself. It is extremely difficult to both be responsible for the meeting's outcomes and be the graphic facilitator. You will find it very difficult to objectively listen. And it is hard to switch gears and go from listening and capturing to speaking up with your input. It is also challenging to be focused on both the process and the content.

It is natural to guide the conversation or the drawing toward the outcome you want. Two ways to counteract this natural inclination is to swap with or brief a colleague:

Swap. Develop your graphic facilitation skills with people in other areas of your company. You will have a cohort to share learnings with and will have coworkers to swap meetings with. You can map your colleague's Human Resource discussion, and later she records your Finance meeting. You can attend your meeting and have it captured by someone with a degree of professional distance.

Brief a colleague on your ideas. They can act as your advocate in the meeting, so you can focus on your role.

While mapping a financial services company's meeting, a participant gestured toward me and asked, "Where did you find her?"

The facilitator deadpanned, "She's from accounting." The group of 80 collectively gasped at the idea that one person could both draw and know accounting.

I looked over my shoulder and shook my head no. They fell into laughter.

When you are a great listener, people assume you are one of them. It's a fantastic compliment. We need to be valued for both our responsiveness to the specific group and our outside perspective.

Not All Speakers are Created Equal

Remember how it is not about you? Yes, it is about the groups you serve. Those groups are populated with human beings. Imperfect human beings.

Some people are better-spoken than others. Some meetings are better-facilitated than others. Remember we are all human.

Beginner graphic facilitators tie themselves up in knots when they make mistakes. Yes, sometimes you do make mistakes. You get distracted with what you need to do the next day. A dried-up marker threw you off course. You go into a trance drawing 3-D block letters. We are human too.

Often the problem is with the speaker. Not everyone is silver-tongued, clear and concise. Some people mumble. Some people ramble. Some people are in over their heads and are speaking in doggie paddle.

Understand that if you're having a problem with what someone is saying, there's a good chance others are too. One person's idea may be hard to capture because it was less-defined. A good facilitator will ask questions on everyone's behalf. "Could you speak up?" or "I'm not sure I understand your point. Can you summarize it?" As the graphic facilitator, you can ask these questions, though sometimes it is difficult to pause your work.

Over time you will hear different types of speakers and learn how to listen and record them. You will better identify when you've missed the mark and when the speaker did. And yes, with experience you can make a muddled speaker or a poorly moderated panel look more cohesive and coherent than it actually was.

A big, three-day annual conference kicked off with an outside keynote speaker. Keynote speakers tend to be expert communicators and well-organized. Not always the case. As this man began, I stood and listened, waiting for him to get into the meat of his talk. Ten minutes into his hour, he hadn't really made any point or set any context. I realized I'd just have to do the best I could. The next 50 minutes felt like three hours as I strained to make connections between his disparate ideas.

I was on a stage along the side wall of a hotel

ballroom filled with 400 people. In that moment, I was thrilled there wasn't a videographer recording me. I got clammy and sweaty. I had 13 years of experience under my belt, and had never heard a speaker be so disjointed and scattered. In the hour he spoke, he never talked about any one idea for more than a minute, and didn't string any of those ideas together.

This was the first time I had worked with this company and it was an awkward start to our three days together.

Mercifully, my lead client came up to me on the break afterwards. She immediately said, "I am so sorry. That was awful." She then looked at the chart and said, "You did a great job with what you had to work with."

I breathed a giant sigh of relief.

It is vital that you capture all the different voices in the room. It is your skill to bring them all together in a cohesive whole.

Here is who I see out in the graphic facilitation wilderness. I describe all these types with a loving heart and the hope that it helps you listen and understand each speaker more fully.

A Field Guide to Speakers

The Keynoter

Characteristics

A single speaker who is given about an hour to share content they know. Quality of communication varies wildly. Some keynoters are organized, clear and have great slides to support their message; others are less organized, more nervous, and read from their slides.

Distinctive Call

"In the next hour I will share with you the results of the Such and Such project." Or, "I am here to share my umpteen years of experience through five key learnings."

How to Capture

Be cautious about numbers. A speaker may begin with, "I've got five points." They may be crystal clear and share five. Or they may skip one, or run out of time. They may share two, but want you to buy the book they are selling and signing to get the other three. Beware of drawing those numbers first. You can always add numbers at the end of a speech for clarity.

Let their slides do their job. You do yours. This goes for anyone projecting slides accompanying their presentation. Do not feel the need to replicate the details of their slides. Their slides and your drawing have two different functions. If an image, quote or diagram from their presentation resonates with the audience, feel free to capture it on your drawing.

The Motivational Speaker

Characteristics

A single speaker who is given about an hour to move an audience to action. Motivational speakers often share their own personal experiences and tell stories to convey their message. Also known as The Storyteller.

Distinctive Call

"Let me share my story of how I got from a Really Lousy Place to a Really Great Place and what I learned along the way."

How to Capture

Capture milestones and destination, not the whole journey. Often these speakers imbue their talks with lots of detail and emotion. Listen for turning points, vivid imagery, key quotes. Map elements of their story that resonate with the audience. Viewing these touchstones later will help viewers fill in the rest of the story.

Leave room for the Big Finish. These speakers will often conclude with a powerful call to action or share the moral of their story. Make sure you have space on your map to highlight their conclusion.

The Boss

Characteristics

The head honcho. The person in the room with the most power and position. They may or may not be your lead point of contact.

Distinctive Call

"We will double our revenue in the next six months."

How to Capture

All voices are equal. Yes, the Boss may have more power overall, but be egalitarian in your mapping. The kind of bosses and leaders who have graphic facilitators in their meetings tend to want to hear all inputs. They do not want their input drawn in a way that overshadows other perspectives.

Separate the objectives. The Boss may kick off the meeting's objectives. Map these on their own sheet of paper or flipchart as a useful reference point throughout the meeting. Keep it hanging in a visible spot in the room. The group can check in throughout the agenda to gauge if they are meeting their objectives.

The Rambler

Characteristics

Someone who takes a long route to get to their point. It could be that they are thinking out loud. It could be that they are unfocused.

Distinctive Call

"What do I think of our customer's experience? Well, it reminds me of what happened last week. I had a problem with my cable. I really was looking forward to..."

How to Capture

Step back and listen. Wait for them to get to their point. Note the details it took to get them there, and map them if they support the conclusion. You need to capture their point, not necessarily all the details that lead up to it.

Ask them to summarize. If they truly rambled away and didn't make a point, ask, "I don't want to miss your point. Can you summarize?" The group is more likely to chide the Rambler, rather than criticize you, since they have heard him or her do this before.

The Mumbler

Characteristics

A speaker who talks in a low or quiet tone that is difficult to hear. The Fader is a variant, someone who starts clear and then trails off. You are not the only person in the room who can't hear The Mumbler. Also known as the Low Talker.

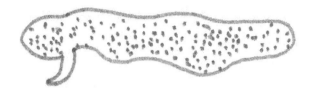

Distinctive Call

"I think we shuh fuzza wuzza hmm...."

How to Capture

Simply say, "I didn't catch that." Again, other people are also straining to here these quiet talkers. You help the group by speaking up for them to speak up.

Use your body language. Convey that you are straining to hear. Move closer to them. Some Mumblers will pick up on the nonverbal clues. Other will remain clueless.

The Parrot

Characteristics

Someone who simply repeats what the previous person said. Possible reasons: Agreement, not paying attention and keeping their cover, new to the group and finding their way, uncertain why they are in the meeting at all.

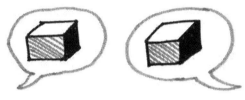

Distinctive Call

"I agree with [insert name of last person to speak]." Or, "All my ideas have been said."

How to capture

Don't. Yes, you should capture everyone's responses. You don't need to write the same thing twice. Underline the point or literally point at the place where it was said before.

The Devil's Advocate

Characteristics

Participants who primarily contribute critical comments and shoot down ideas. Also known as Naysayer, or Wet Blanket. Devil's Advocates are dismissed for just being negative. While some *are* simply negative, most are critical because they want to strengthen the solution to the problem. Seeing that they are being heard, they are some of the more responsive to graphic facilitation.

Distinctive Call

"Yeah, but I don't see how that could work." Or, "We tried that five years ago and got nowhere."

How to Capture

Put a generative spin on their comment. Word their idea in a way that keeps the conversation going and solutions coming, instead of shutting it down. They may say, "We tried that five years ago. It didn't work" Reframe it as "What have we learned since we tried this last?" or "How will we make this succeed this time?"

Don't feed the trolls. Capture a criticism or negative comment once. If a Naysayer gets stuck in a negative loop, there is no need to keep reiterating their comment on the map. At most underline the idea if they repeat it, or point at it to show it's been captured.

The Emotional
Characteristics
Like the Devil's Advocate, emotional speakers tend to be tamped down within a company's culture for being too touchy-feely. They are especially responsive to seeing their often-dismissed message be listened to. The Emotional tend to tap into motivations: the Why behind the What or How. Passionate people tend to help define purpose and vision.

Distinctive Call
"I cannot believe we've been talking data the last two hours. What I care about is the experience of our patrons and if we help them grow and learn."

How to Capture
Quote them. Get their passionate quote up on the board, linked to the ideas and details in supports.

Promote the purpose. Often these speakers' contributions connect to broader themes, or get to underlying issues. These comments are often bigger scale within the conversation than supporting details. If appropriate, write these comments larger or set them apart in a banner or box.

The Outlier

Yes, all voices are equal in a meeting, but the Outlier appears to be in another meeting altogether.

[In a conversation about human resource issues] "Have we thought about making our packaging biodegradable?"

Don't capture it. If they are truly having another conversation altogether, don't map the comment. You can also put it on a sticky note near your chart. If the group comes around to the Outlier's topic, you can integrate the note into the map.

The Detail-Oriented Person

Characteristics

These are speakers who adore the details. They swim happily in data. They are often less capable of making conclusions from the details.

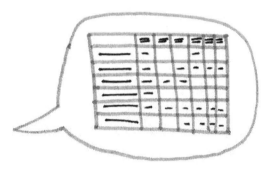

Distinctive Call

"If you look at page 7, column 4, second row down, you'll see our profits in this sector rose 2%."

How to Capture

Record conclusions from the data, not the data itself. Your role is not to recreate tables. Most people will have handouts of the information. Listen for the group's reaction to the data and the key learnings from the numbers.

Highlight a resonant piece of data. When one statistic or number gets repeated, capture it. If a 30% drop in the third quarter is seen as the team's turning point, get in on the map.

The Big Picture Person

Characteristics

The complement to The Detail-Oriented, these participants excel at sharing the themes and conclusions of the group. Often, these folks are the graphic facilitator's favorite. Also known as The Summarizer.

Distinctive Call

"I'm hearing two big themes here..." Or, "What I think the group is saying is..."

How to Capture

Watch for response. Watch for a group's agreement with their colleague's summary.

Highlight or set apart the summary. These inputs are about seeing themes, understanding context and reaching conclusions. These types of content are often drawn in a bigger scale, highlighted or set apart in banners or boxes.

Connect the wrap-up to what it is wrapping up. The Big Picture Person is responding to details from earlier in the conversation. Place their observations close to the source and be sure to show the connections.

115

The Metaphor Fan

Characteristics

A speaker who works through their ideas using metaphors and analogous thinking.

Distinctive Call

"I see this annual report as a tree...." Or, "Ah, this is like..."

How to Capture

Watch the group. See if the speaker's metaphor is working for the group. Listen for multiple people using the metaphor and building on it.

Don't latch onto imagery. Inexperienced graphic facilitators jump at the chance to draw metaphorical imagery. At worst, they hear "tree" and draw one three feet tall, when it may have only been a passing point.

Capture the idea in an icon. If metaphor resonates, make it more prominent. There's no real harm in drawing both a three-inch tall tree icon to capture the idea first and then later a three-foot tall tree when the group embraces it as the metaphor that explains everything ever.

The Architect

Characteristics

A speaker who thinks structurally and communicates in models and images.

Distinctive Call

"I see where this conversation is going. I'm seeing our foundational message with three pillars on it. The first is X, the second Y, the third Z."

How to Capture

Watch the group. Make sure their model is making sense. The Metaphor Fan, the Architect and the Big Picture Person are making useful and astute observations worth capturing. Gauging response helps you better know how to treat it on the map.

Ask them to show you a sketch. Most described models are fairly simple, but if it is more complicated, ask them to show you. Very likely, they've already drawn it while they were listening and forming the idea.

You can ask them to draw it on the map themselves. While I welcome their addition to my work, participants resist. They sense an imaginary force field, that it's my map and off limits. Very few people will break that field.

Keep it simple. The Architects of the group aren't usually describing ornate palaces in their mind. They are thinking of a simple scaffolding to help summarize the conversation and take the group's thinking farther. It's good to draw these images simply, because the group may respond with changes and additions.

Distill

You are not a stenographer. It is impossible to hand-write a conversation verbatim. And even if you could, you shouldn't. You listen to all the words being said; you distill those words into key ideas.

This is a glass vessel called a retort.* Used for distilling liquids, heat is applied to the round base of the retort. The vapors rise. Those gases cool down and travel down the neck. The resulting liquid is the distillation. Take a look at the retort as a metaphor for your role as a listener in your client's meeting:

*Thank you to John Ward for sharing this retort metaphor.

119

Throughout the book, I direct you to "capture everything in the meeting." Truly, you are capturing all the salient points that condense in the neck of the retort. A lot of the liquid of the conversation is: ramping up to an idea; giving context around an idea; agreement; hems and haws; side conversations; and levity. The distillation is: the key points; the ideas; useful details around ideas; feedback to the ideas; important questions; and resonant quotes.

If you were truly capturing all the words, your clients would have to filter out all the unimportant components. You distill the conversation on their behalf.

In Practice

Be accurate with the group's language. A food company may be discussing "encased meats" and you write "sausages." That label of sausages may be distracting because they officially label that part of their business Encased Meats.

This is held in balance with:

Reduce jargon. Your use of clearer language helps facilitate the group. For instance, the client may say their customers want new encased meats. Well, the average consumer would never say that. They want sausages. Experience will help you navigate this path.

Keep a generative lens. You want the text you capture to both reflect on the conversation and keep it going. Negative comments should be worded so they invite conversation, not close it down. A Devil's Advocate says, "Our vendors won't work with us." Put a generative spin on it by writing, "New ways to work with our vendors?" That keeps the group focused on solutions.

Drop articles. Instead of "President of the United States" write "US President."

Drop useless adjectives. "A tattered, billowing American Flag" can be simplified to "American flag." Yes, some adjectives are useful. Filter out the ones that don't carry their weight.

Don't name names. Anonymity in ideas is very useful in creating a group's shared understanding. Personally, the only time I write names down is at the end of meetings, when people are committing to specific follow-up work or next steps.

Use symbols and abbreviations. An up or down arrow can connote more of one thing, less of another. "w/" is speedier than "with." "Re:" in reference to something. "ex" for example.

THINKING

Let's think about thinking, shall we?

As we look at thinking skills in the context of graphic facilitation, we are guided by six Principles. Here is how they relate:

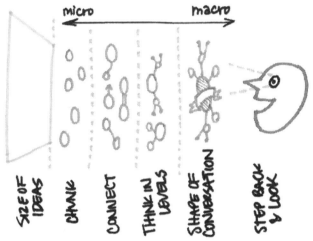

To begin, you choose the surface you'll be drawing on with the **Size of Ideas**. Last, you **Step Back & Look** at your work. In between are four ways to think about the conversation you're listening to, moving from micro to macro. First, you listen to the conversation for the individual pieces, **Chunking** of information. Second, you think about how each new chunk **Connects** or doesn't connect to what is already on your map. Third, you **Think in Levels**, using scale, color, line and shape to further organize the chunks of information. Fourth, you consider the **Shape of Conversation**, anticipating and adapting to what the group says.

Size of Ideas

The first decision in graphic facilitation is the size of paper you'll be using. Consider the size of work to be done. Consider the time you have. Most importantly, think about the size of ideas you are working on.

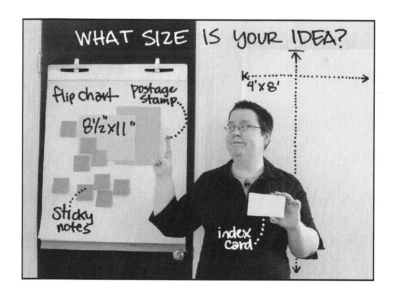

We are surrounded by paper, most of it plain old, boring Mr. Letter-Sized. We relate to him in piles on our desks, portrait-orientation, filled with text. And if he's wearing his pinstripes, he keeps us thinking in a linear way.

Nowadays the Boring Mister has a wife, Mrs. Flipchart. She didn't take his last name. Just as we've become overly accustomed to letter-sized paper, we're comfortably numb with flipcharts. And they had tons of sticky note babies. I don't mean to be too hard on them; they are a lovely, accessible couple.

 Remember that these are the formats which are so ever-present that we take them for granted; we think of them in the same ways whenever we see them.

Think about the size of paper you choose and how much it challenges your thinking. Or doesn't. There is something a little new and dangerous about walking up to a 4-foot x 8-foot piece of paper. Where will you draw? What will you draw?

What would happen if you recorded on hundreds of 3-inch by 5-inch cards? What if you drew a key idea the size of a postage stamp? What if you tiled a wall with 12-inch square pieces? Used round pieces of paper? How would you approach the conversation differently? How would the information be split up or pieced together?

In Practice

Make familiar materials feel less familiar. Even if you have letter-sized paper, turn it 90 degrees. Or tear it in half to give yourself a different shape and size. Hang a flipchart paper horizontally.

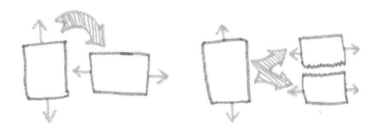

Go large. Most graphic facilitators work on large sheets of paper, roughly four feet tall and six to eight feet long. This giant format allows a generous amount of space for a conversation. A large roll of paper takes some practice to handle. Some people like pre-cutting their paper to make work easier onsite. Others keep their paper intact on the rolls to make it easier to adapt to the site.

Give yourself options. Even if you work on a giant sheet of paper, have a flipchart nearby. It is very handy: jot a quick list, make a summary of your large chart, write down team names, etc.

Look at the agenda for ideas. The agenda and a conversation with your client or facilitator will help you gauge what size paper will work best for the length of conversation and the process.

If I have very little information, I can still gauge that in a day I can easily make four charts, if the whole group is in plenary (not breaking out into groups). One chart before the first break, another before lunch, a third one between lunch and the afternoon break and a fourth chart before the meeting adjourns.

Notice "real estate." As you gain experience, note how much paper you use in a given time and with a given process. Be mindful and you'll better gauge how much paper you will need in the future.

Chunk

Chunking is the ability to listen to a conversation and pull out individual pieces of information. Chunking is harvesting the relevant points from what is extraneous, sorting the gems from the gibble gabble.*

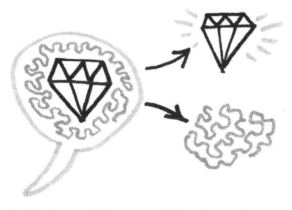

Gems include a point, a new idea, important context, feedback on an existing idea, useful variations on a comment or idea, a quote, a pertinent piece of data or an anecdote that reinforces a point. Gibble gabble is all the other conversation around the gems: unnecessary detail, side talk, hemming and hawing,

*Thanks to Lynn Carruthers for her term "gibble gabble."

build-up before a point. Much gibble gabble is useful in the spoken conversation for transitions between ideas or how people are relating to each other face-to-face. It's only gibble gabble because it doesn't need to be recorded on the chart.

Gems are the chunks that need to go up on your chart. Think of a chunk as the smallest unit of conversational measure. Chunking goes hand-in-hand with distilling language. You listen for a chunk of conversation and then distill its wording down to the most salient point.

In Practice

Chunk hunt. Outside of projects, listen to conversations with a focus on what the chunks are. Read a paragraph listing the chunks. Generally a sentence is a chunk, but many sentences are supporting chunks or summary chunks.

Unbundle chunks. Someone could say, "We need to make our public programs more relevant, increase visitor numbers and improve member incentives." While that is one sentence, it is three different chunks:

more relevant public programs

↑ increase visitor numbers

improve member incentives

Separating each chunk makes it easier to connect later chunks to any of those three ideas.

Don't judge chunks. Someone offers a point and then another person contradicts their point or shuts it down. Capture the initial point. Add the criticism (with a generative spin) alongside it. This reflects both of those chunks within the whole conversation.

For example, after the previous speaker's point, someone replies, "Our public programs aren't getting us anywhere." That doesn't mean you cross out the initial point. The conversation continues and the group decides:

more relevant
public programs

measure
pub. programs
against visitor
& member #'s

Connect

Once you get great at hunting chunks, you can connect them to each other.

The bulk of what you do as a graphic facilitator is to listen for the next chunk of conversation and think about where to place it in relation to what has already been said. You draw those connections in a meaningful way. Chunking and connecting build up into drawings that represent the whole conversation.

Generally, when someone makes a point, that is a chunk. The next comment could be agreement to the first chunk, a supporting point for the first chunk, a main point for which the first chunk is supporting, or a new point/chunk.

Connections or Relationships Between Chunks

One idea is a single chunk.

Two ideas that are **similar** to each other can be placed closed together.

Two **dissimilar** ideas can be placed further apart from each other.

A **connection** between two ideas can be shown with a line between them.

A **strong connection** can be represented with a thicker line.

A dotted line works well for a **possible or weak connection**.

Large & small ideas can be drawn in proportion to each other, with different sizes of text or shapes.

Scale, close proximity and a connecting line can show a **main** idea and **supporting** ideas branching off of it.

Ideas that **feed into** another one can be represented with directional arrows and placement before the main idea.

Conversely, ideas that are the **products from** a main idea can have arrows point out of the main idea and the products listed after it.

Arrows easily create **direction**.

Multiple ideas on a path with arrows create **flow**.

Two ideas that share qualities are represented with shapes that **overlap**.

Several ideas that closely relate make **groupings**, well represented when enclosed within a dotted or solid line.

A **hierarchy** represents items ranked above and below other items in a pyramidal, vertical shape. Hierarchies have a top and bottom.

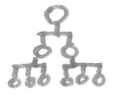 

A **holarchy** is a nested organizational form where each level is both a whole and a part of the next larger level.

A **heterarchy** is made up of interconnected nodes in a web. While a heterarchy can contain hierarchies, they tend to represent horizontal relationship instead of vertical ones.

In Practice

Practice making connections. Like chunk hunting, you get better at making connections with practice. Outside of the pressure of events, listen to conversations, interviews or podcasts, focusing on how different ideas relate to each other.

Listen for spatial clues. Often people preface their comments with useful context. "That idea reminds me of..." sounds like she's sharing a similar idea. "I want to build on that" is a point that supports an existing point. "I want to switch gears," signals a new, dissimilar idea. "Can we go back to something before?" references an earlier topic to connect to.

Think in Levels

Not all information lives on the same level. Your charts should be organized to clearly reflect both main topics and their supporting points. **Chunking** and **Connecting** feed into this. Later, you'll use **The Essential Eight** to draw how each point clearly relates to the others using color, line, scale, shapes and iconography.

Thinking in layers means thinking critically to organize what is being said in the meeting, to help everyone make more meaning of their work. As we said in **Listen with Outsider Ears**, everyone is equal. Not every idea is equal. There is a tension here.

Most of this book lives in the tidy isolation of an imaginary meeting. It is useful to temporarily give a broader context.

I'm going to grossly over-summarize my Art History education to make a point. And this goes far beyond fine art. As I prefaced in **I Am Your Guide**, I am a practitioner, not a scholar, so I hope you'll cut me some slack, and forgive me no citations.

In the late-19th Century, Modernism made a few people (mostly old, rich, white men) the only voices worth listening to. There is One Truth.

In response, Postmodernism arose mid-20th Century, giving voice to everyone (young and old, any class level, any race or background, any gender or sexual orientation). Truth is Subjective. There are Many Truths.

Postmodernism has been incredibly empowering, putting everyone on egalitarian, equal footing. It's a fantastically powerful thing that we have access to different perspectives and can speak up for ourselves and hear all these different voices.

The consequence is that there are now infinite voices out there to listen to— amplified by new technologies. It is that firehose of information, channels, user comments and status updates we are soaked with daily. We are in a transition into Post-Postmodernism or whatever we're going to call it. (I enjoy calling it PoPoMo). We struggle to understand all the inputs we receive and how to make sense of them.

Postmodernism tells us every voice is valid. And each is.

 AND we must organize these voices, understand them in context, filter them for specific uses and find voices and sources we trust.

In this transition into the 21st Century, we hold onto the values that all voices are equal, while struggling with how to listen and understand all those voices at once. We need to develop PoPoMo tools to listen to everyone, understand context, think critically and organize information to make it usable.

All those voices aren't useful if we are exhausted by them and we just plug our ears.

The Graphic Facilitation field grew up alongside Postmodernism. First wave graphic facilitators hold the democracy and equality very strongly, resulting in charts of ideas all living on one level. Forty years into this work, I posit that we live in a world that needs the next wave of graphic facilitators to incorporate more organization and synthesis into their work. It is alright to separate the input from the person who said it. We can add structure to these inputs without invalidating the sources. In fact, the structure helps all the participants see their perspectives and how to relate to each other. As graphic facilitators, we can sort, rank and connect ideas without devaluing them. In fact this sorting, ranking and connecting adds value to the meeting itself by creating more shared meaning.

I believe graphic facilitation is a 21st century role that helps us navigate this complex world we live in. Graphic facilitation is an adaptable, accessible and powerful PoPoMo tool. Organizing and synthesizing skills are rarely taught, are very difficult to teach, and hadn't been supported in the Postmodern context. If you feel uncomfortable with these skills, know that they are new territory for most people. But they are, alongside critical thinking, very much in demand.

We'll now return to our tidy little imaginary meeting, after this context setting. We can believe both that all voices are valid and that not all ideas are equal.

We build on our abilities to listen, distill, chunk and connect. Once we can evaluate, sort, scale and organize ideas apart from the people who share them, we can **Think in Layers**.

Here's a sample hunk (assembly of chunks) with five layers:

Level 1: A category written in large, uppercase letters.

Level 2: Items within that category connect with stems from the category's box. Drawn in smaller text in lowercase letters.

Level 3: Details that support individual items. Even smaller text and lowercase letters. These are connected to their responding items with lines.

Level 4: A quote that reinforces the grouping of ideas or the category. It's drawn within a speech bubble.

Level 5: A theme that summaries a collection of items or details. It is drawn in uppercase letters in a ribbon to wrap around the details it describes and set it apart.

Thinking in Layers involves identifying chunks as different types of information (category, item, detail, quote, theme).

Here's how you visually organize those layers of information:

Make Choices.

Hopefully chunking and connecting is making the graphic facilitation process feel less daunting. And that you anticipate thinking in levels to organize different types of information.

You can help yourself further by making choices up front. Build on your previous experience and make some design decisions before you put pen to paper. Examples:

"I'm mapping this chart in red, orange and black, and highlighting with yellow."

"I'm marking each of the key insights with a ."

"As I hear quotes that resonate, I'll capture them in this area of my chart, each within its own light blue quote bubble."

"Whenever the group discusses branding, I will use their brand's color of green to reinforce the message."

Constraints can free you. Once you know the givens of a situation, you can work within them. Not only does this free you from fumbling with a bunch of markers, you are creating patterns of colors, shapes and symbols in your chart that reflect patterns in the conversation. People look for similarities, or rather, they notice what's dissimilar.

In our sample above, each of the five levels is drawn a certain way: upper- or lowercase letters, size of letters, types of connectors, each contained in different shapes.

Once you make these choices:

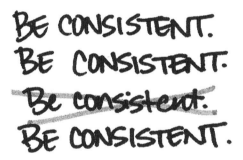

Each of the five sample levels is drawn consistently. Each detail is the same size and same relative scale and distance from the item it supports.

Break your rules when you mean it. If your red, orange and yellow chart's conversation takes a left turn, add new colors for the new topic.

Adding a New Layer

Often in meetings, we fill charts with conversation. Tons of ideas get up on the wall and tons of work gets done. Sometimes the group needs to step back and look at their work and make decisions from it. The group builds on their shared understanding by selecting and merging ideas.

It is helpful to show that decision-making process on your charts. You can use a new color to circle and highlight the ideas that rise to the top. You can create a new list on a flipchart next to the original chart. You can give participants dot stickers and let people "dot vote" for their favorite ideas. Here, each big idea is marked with a star. This makes a logical landing pad for the dot stickers:

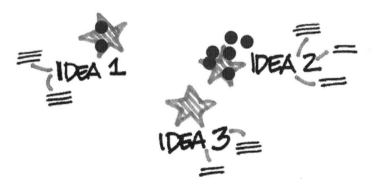

Shape of Conversation

Every conversation has its own shape. I am often asked, "How do you know where the conversation is going to go?"

I don't. I start with a large, blank sheet of paper and respond to and reflect what is being said in the room. There are three keys:

- You don't know where the conversation is going to go.

- You give yourself places to go.

- Everyone watches the drawing take shape together.

Give Yourself Places to Go

A lot of work out there is fundamentally linear, like this:

This chart makes it look like the conversation is seven pieces that all happened in a tidy, linear order. Like this:

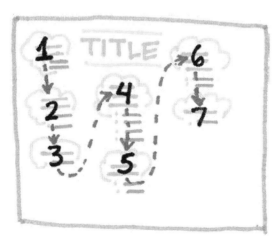

I don't know many conversations that really happen that way. The group may talk about topic 1, then 2, then 3 then 4, then someone adds a point to 1. Or connects point 4 to 3.

If you map in this linear way your charts will be very, very tidy, but are unlikely to reflect how organic and interconnected the conversation is. Let's hope these thinking principles of **Chunking, Connecting** and **Thinking in Layers** already are shifting your approach away from going the linear route and toward giving yourself new places to go.

One very simple way to give yourself places to go is to work from the center. It may feel risky to start in the center of the page, but you are rewarded with more flexibility.

Think of the chart as a pie cut into slices. You can put the main topics near the center. Then you get the opportunity to work out from the center like this:

The pie slices get wider, giving you more places to go. You are less likely to draw yourself into a corner.

A prep call with your facilitator or client will help you anticipate the shape of the conversation. If you know the group will answer three questions in the next hour, you can divide your chart in thirds. At most, lightly pencil in these divisions, since the agenda and conversation can always change.

Over time you'll recognize more shapes that conversations tend to take, like horizontal maps built around timelines, or charts with vertical pieces as a group discusses parallel actions.

Use Anchors and Lassos

There are two basic ways to label a topic:

Make it an anchor at the beginning of the conversation   **Put a lasso around it afterwards**

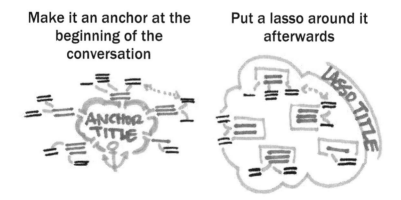

You can start a chart with the title. This is a useful security blanket for people when they start out. It gives you a chance to begin drawing while you listen. It helps some folks warm up. Be careful to not to use up too much space with the title.

You can cluster all the content around that central title. Again, you can expand out and are less likely to draw yourself into a corner.

Conversely, you can make your map and label it afterwards. You can make a thick line lasso around all the pieces under a topic.

Generally speaking, anchors and lassos create two types of images:

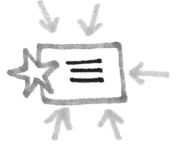

A central anchor allows the shape of the conversation to expand out. These feel open, still in progress, generative.

Putting a lasso, box or shape around a grouping constricts a topic. These shapes feel contained, fixed, finished, complete.

Everyone Watches the Drawing Take Shape Together

Yes, I've had projects where I made something like this:

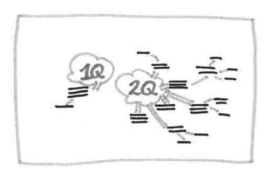

Two questions are asked, one gets answered immediately and definitively. The other sparks an hour-long conversation.

I've also had charts that looked like this:

I was told there was going to be an hour on a topic and time gets cut short. Or I encountered a panel discussion where 80% of the time was spent introducing the panelists, with surprisingly little discussion.

Everyone was there. They heard the same lengthy panelist introductions and how little they talked about the subject itself.

Assuming you did capture the content and didn't freeze up, it is all right if the shape of the conversation is a strange, lopsided shape.

The process is adaptive. You are responding to the group, and they are responding to you. Everyone is watching the image being created. They know exactly where it came from because they watched you draw it.

Shaping the Conversation: Templates

This guide focuses on facilitating the group by rolling out a giant, blank sheet of paper and listening to what they say, observing what they do. Nothing is more adaptable than that clean canvas. You map their open-ended conversation and the group feels the power of being listened to.

Another direction to take this work is to create templates. In these cases you work with your facilitator and client to create the shape of the conversation beforehand and design a template that you, the participants or the facilitator fills in.

The right template, designed the right way at the right time, can be very useful. There are two main dangers to templates: Not having the right template, and fill-in-the-box thinking.

Prepared templates are hard to adapt if the meeting's needs change. In the rare cases I have created templates for events, they have been created spontaneously and hand-drawn onsite. This also forces them to be very simple and not too polished. Templates should be as unrefined as possible in style to prevent them from being unapproachable. A computer-drawn, laminated template looks slick and is also very intimidating. A hand-drawn template on common flipchart paper feels more accessible.

Templates have a predetermined shape. Say a template has five areas to fill. Pre-made graphics do help your participants consider all five of those areas. It also makes them think only of those five areas. The assignment of filling in a template restricts their thinking to what is in front of them, and people may not address what's not on the template.

If you want to shape the conversation with the templates, carefully design the shape of the template to fit the meeting's needs and the style of the template (scale, materials and hand-drawn or computer-drawn) that will be used.

In Practice

Look at the agenda. While it is important to let the shape of the conversation emerge, look at the agenda for clues to the shape of the agenda. A conversation may be designed around three questions, or three key groups of people. You could anticipate drawing three groupings of ideas. Again, adapt your drawing to the conversation. Do not force your idea of the shape onto what is being said.

Mapping a session about the beginnings of the graphic facilitation industry at the 15th annual conference of the International Forum of Visual Practitioners. As the speakers were introduced, I drew a giant bow and 15 to represent the celebration. The ribbon-like arrows extend from the bow creating a timeline. I placed the central drawing off center, to give two-thirds of the chart to talking about the past. The remaining third could hold talk of the future, or could have been left blank if the group had not discussed it. Part of the finished drawing:

Step Back & Look

We work large scale. And we often stay within arm's length of the paper. We stay so close to our work that we don't see it from the group's perspective.

Step Back and Look. Move around the room and see how the chart looks from the middle of the room, the back.

When we are too close to our own work, a lot of our charts look like this:

All the content is small and on the same level. It may be surprisingly hard to read from not very far away. Everything looks like a scattered handful of popcorn.

As you develop your skills and use these six thinking Principles, your charts will hopefully look more like this:

You can read more from a distance. You can see layers of organization.

As I said in **Be Seen**, we can't accommodate every person's eyesight in the room. But we do need to **Step Back and Look** and get beyond our own point of view.

In Practice

Step back and look during breaks. Don't step away in the middle of conversation. Moving away from your role in the moment will disrupt the group. If you want to get a different perspective live, simply:

Squint.

Frequently step back and look. Stop several times a day, over the course of a multiple-day project. Do the charts look different from each other? Following **Content is King,** are you using color or drawing motifs to help differentiate one map from another aligned with the content?

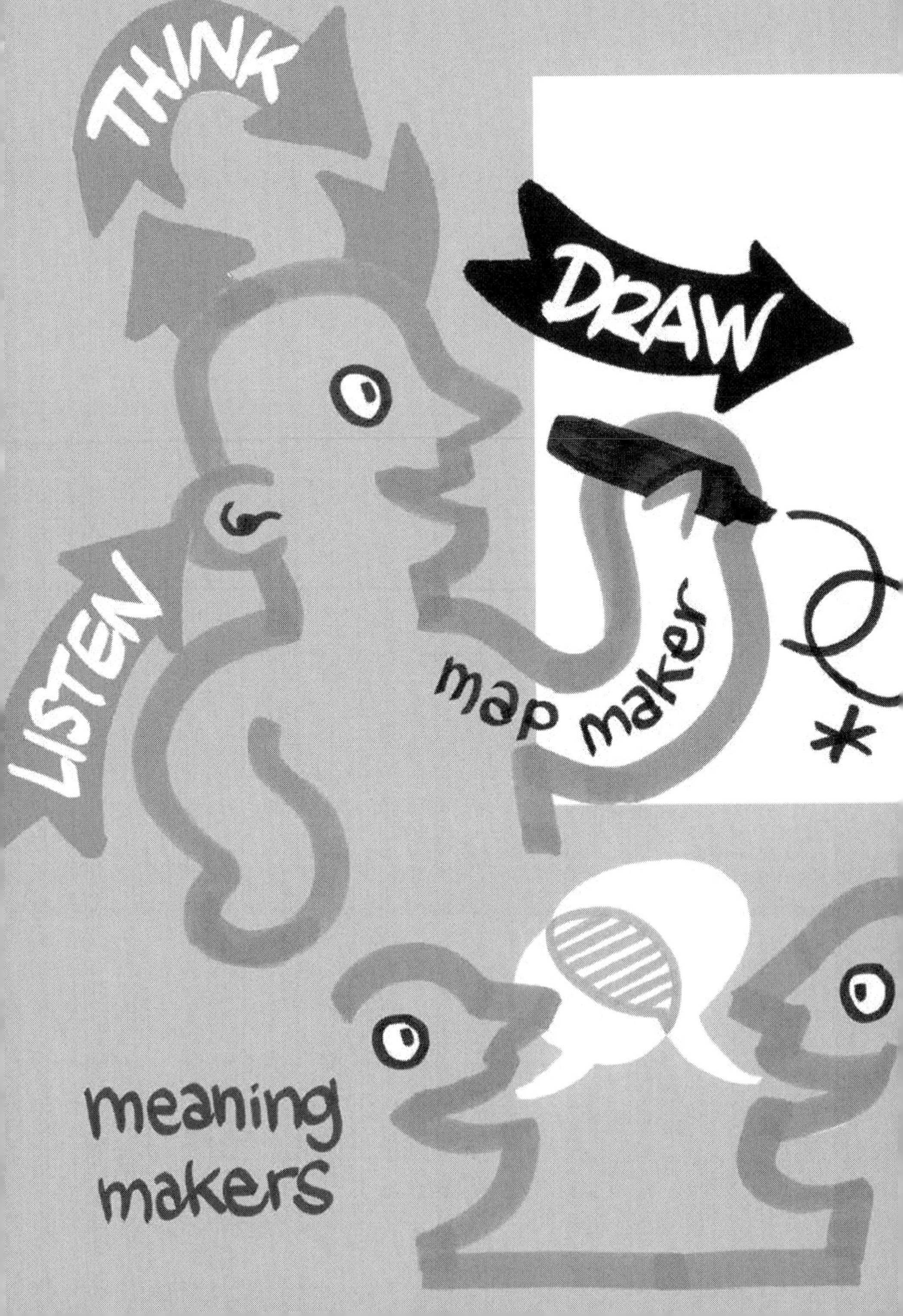
THINK
DRAW
LISTEN
map maker
meaning makers

DRAWING

meeting maker

Every Mark has Meaning

We as human beings are meaning making machines. We look for meaning in every bit of input our senses take in. Every mark we make has meaning.

The presence of a graphic facilitator serving a group enables that group to see their work take shape. It makes the ephemeral, temporal act of conversation concrete, captured on paper. The transparency and tangibility of these drawings allow all participants to view their conversation from a new perspective. You add a new element to the proceedings and you're adding a new way for everyone to make meaning.

All eyes look to you. Your participants watch you to see their conversation reflected back to them. In every marker stroke is the opportunity to aid and support them. In every marker stroke is the possibility to distract and confuse them. Even if you as a graphic facilitator make a meaningless mark, your participants will be looking for meaning in it.

Don't let this scare you. You are 80% alright, 80% of the time. Just be aware of a few things as you go to "tighten up" the other 20%.

Now, let's make a mark—

Ways to Make Marks Meaningful

Form
First you make the shape. What is this? We know it's a curve that opens to the left with a bit of a vertical stem.

Quality of Line
The type of line you use to draw the shape contributes to the meaning. This shape could be a wispy line for smoke—

Or a strong line, like a heavy-duty hanger to hang your winter coat on.

Color
Choice of color gives clues to meaning. Here our shape is pink and becomes a bald man's ear.

Placement
If we duplicate our shape and make it a mirror image, now our marks make a chef's hat.

166

Orientation

Turning the shape opens up our mark to new meaning. Now it could be a ladle.

Or a round, cartoon nose. Or a hook to hang your favorite mug on.

Or a hill. Or a pompadour. Or a hilly pompadour.

Proximity

Where a mark sits in relationship to other marks gives a mark meaning. I don't know what that mark is, but I can tell it has a closer relationship to the blobby shape than the square.

Detail

Adding more marks to your initial mark helps it make sense. Now our mark is a chunky, bold, 3-D question mark for The Big Question.

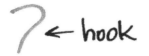

Label

Marks can be friends with text. A label can clearly define an ambiguous mark.

In Practice

Make meaningful marks. You can draw a face and give it meaning through simple marks:

Make *every* mark meaningful. I personally don't use my time to embellish an image. I will add details to an image only when those details make the image's meaning more clear.

Make choices and be consistent. We already covered this territory, but it bears repeating. Be consistent in your choices. People pick up on inconsistencies and wonder why the exception was made.

Be confident in your line. Make bold marks, even if they aren't perfect. Broken, hesitant marks will make the group uneasy, along with nervous body language. Even if you are new and need to act, be confident. People will forgive some wonkiness in your work if it is done with ease. My work can definitely be wonky sometimes, but it is never nervous.

Complete your shapes. Not every mark you make needs to be fastidious, but they should be well-formed and complete. Here are two examples:

This is a fine box grounding the person. Because the rectangle isn't complete—

It may distract the viewer as the "energy" inside the shape can leak out of the open shape.

This figure stands on a ball, but the top left edge and the top right edge, don't line up—

Viewers may be distracted by this incongruity. Their mind will try to redraw the line.

Granted, some participants are more visually sensitive than others. One person may go nuts seeing a crooked picture frame on the wall, but not care when they see an apostrophe when its misused. Others are made crazy by the last sentence's mistake, but aren't bothered by the misshapen circle above. As a graphic facilitator, you want to minimize all distracting marks, both the open rectangle and the apostrophe.

On the eve of leading a intermediate graphic facilitation workshop in Germany, I got to see my colleagues finish up their beginner's workshop. I watched the participants share their final charts. I last studied German in high school, nearly 20 years ago. I listened with very rusty ears.

One participant had draw a chart with five sections descending vertically in a zig zag:

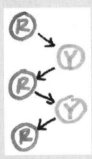

He had drawn the left side items in red, and the right side ones in yellow. Immediately, I wondered why the left and ride side were color-coded. I could see the questioning expressions on his colleagues' faces. One asked him why it was color-coded.

It turns out he was simply alternating between two colors and hadn't realized that they lined up that way. It was illuminating watching this happen through a language barrier, watching the body language as people were uncomfortable trying to make the drawing choices and the content make sense with each other.

The class got an opportunity to discuss this and I was happy they had this mini case study so early in their work. Fewer questioning faces in their futures.

When we first discuss the skills of graphic facilitation, we describe this role as being equal parts listening, thinking and drawing:

Now we'll break down the components of drawing in a way that will keep you in balance. Do not fall into the drawing trap:

It is understandable that drawing is the most intimidating part of this work. I am your guide, and yes, I do come from a drawing background. I can tell you that the vast majority of graphic facilitators come from the people side, not the drawing side. In fact, I see many practitioners from art, design and illustration let the drawing take over. They get caught up in the product over the process. They need to unlearn their drawing skills, because their current skills aren't **Quick Like a Bunny**, or they lose sight of **Content is King**.

Let's break down drawings into these components: **The Essential Eight**. This is drawing within the context of graphic facilitation.

The Essential Eight

LETTERING

Perfectly legible
Drawn fast!

BULLETS

Make separate points clear
Color & symbol coding

COLOR

Bright & inviting
Used to organize

LINE

Connect & contain ideas
Delineate with thick &
thin lines

ARROWS

Guide attention
Create flow & movement

PEOPLE

Bring life to work
Express emotion

BOXES

Highlight & sets apart
Group a set of ideas
together

SHADING

Lift Items off the page
Add dimension

The Essential Eight are sequential. Each element builds on the next. I want you to master lettering before you move onto bullets. This may sound simplistic, boring or didactic. It works. I have had fast-paced projects where all I was doing was using lettering, color and line. I served my client very well without any real iconography. I have seen beginners stall in a meeting, making drop shadow on block letters, and lose the conversation. I have seen folks who are fantastic illustrators with lousy handwriting.

If you are looking for a way to practice, start early in **The Essential Eight**. Build from up from there. If your brain short circuits in the middle of a meeting, go back to square one, to ground yourself and get back on track.

Let's begin!

I had a huge project with chefs testing new food concepts. We worked together for many days in many kitchens. As each of the chef teams revealed their concepts, I was ready at a flipchart. Each concept got its own flipchart page. I captured the chefs' ideas and the taste testers' responses and questions. These flew by. Many charts like these were drawn in less than five minutes.

With very little drawing in these flipcharts, they served the clients well. I used color, line and scale to organize the ideas. Simple faces captured the quick reactions.

These concepts accumulated over a series of events. I used the same structure for each concept, so it was very easy for the client to remember and compare one concept to the next. Because each concept was its own map, the chefs could easily sort them, remove the weaker ideas and prioritize the stronger ones.

Let's look at **The Essential Eight**. Each step ends with a sample chart using all the components up to that point.

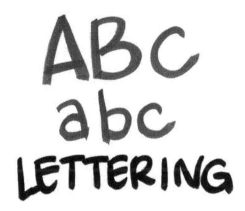

LETTERING

Perfectly legible
Drawn fast!

You may be thinking, "What? Lettering is writing. Not drawing."

Think of lettering as drawing 52 shapes impeccably, 26 uppercase and 26 lowercase letters. Of course, adjust the number to the language you're working in.

I say impeccably. I should say as impeccably as the time allows. **The key to lettering is finding your perfect intersection between legibility and speed.**

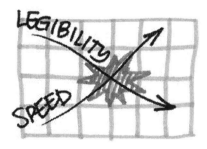

Your letters needs to be legible and you need to write fast. There is always a tradeoff of one for the other.

Stop. Grab a few sheets of scratch paper and a marker. If you're feeling fancy, fold or mark the paper into thirds. Draw an uppercase and lowercase alphabet as you normally would in the first third. In the next third, draw as fast as you can. In the final third, draw for best legibility.

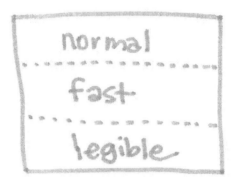

Now hold your paper at arm's length or tape it to a wall and step back.

What do you see or notice?

How legible is each alphabet?

Which letters work and which letters need work?

THIS IS MY FASTWORKING WRITING

MY SLOW/FAST IN·BETWEEN WRITING.

MY SLOW & CAREFUL WRITING.

My Scribbly personal writing

My loopy card-signing writing;

I ♥ BLOCK LETTERS.

I earned an "Insufficient" in penmanship in first grade. No, really.

Next, write an alphabet very slowly. Notice exactly how you write your letters. How many strokes does each letter take? How many times do you pick up your pen? Every stroke drawn and every time you pick up your pen takes time.

You may find there are letters that can be drawn quicker with fewer strokes. This is why I draw my Y's like this:

You may find there are letters that could use an additional stroke to make them more legible. This is why I add the "roof" to my a's. When I'm drawing fast, that extra stroke makes my a's look distinctly different from my o's or u's.

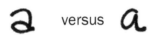

This exercise of dissecting and correcting your handwriting may feel tedious at first. If you practice your corrections, they will come easily to you. You will improve your legibility and speed. This work up front will shave time off of each letter and adds up in the long run. While this work grabs attention for being visual, spatial, colorful, it still involves a ton of writing.

I give myself a B or B– in legibility, but I always get an A for speed.

Consistency is key. Like we said in **Think in Levels** and **Every Mark Has Meaning**, your viewers are always noticing similarities and differences, even on the itty bittiest level. Make your letters consistent.

Once you have your 52 shapes down, you can learn how to change them for different purposes.

 First is using relative letter size. Write bigger ideas in bigger letters, smaller supporting ideas in smaller lettering.

Next use uppercase letter for main points, headers and themes, and lowercase for details and supporting points.

Last is lettering style, going beyond basic printed letters for specific effect. Fancy lettering is tons of fun to draw. It is rarely truly needed. Never forget that **Content is King** and always be **Quick Like a Bunny**.

When it comes to your lettering style, and in turn your drawing style, know your audience. Some graphic facilitator styles look well-suited for an elementary school classroom, other styles look well-suited for a Fortune 500 boardroom. You can have your own style. It will attract a certain audience. You may want to modify your style to appeal to the audience you want to work with. Meet in the middle.

MECHANICAL
DRAWING

BLOCK

SWOOSH

BUBBLES

kindergarten

whisper

You don't need
serifs to make
flipcharts easier
to read.

In Practice

Pick up the pen. The more you pick up your pen between letters and words, the more legible the work. Look at my samples for where letters connect with each other. Picking up the pen adds time, so find the right tradeoff between fast and legible. This is why cursive is not the friend of the graphic facilitator.

Limit entry and exit strokes. These are the tails we add to our letters, left over from learning cursive. Unlearning these habits will give you cleaner, more legible letters.

a not *a*   *t* not *t*

Stay level. As you write left to right, shift your weight from your left leg to your right. This will keep your letters level. We often move from our elbow or shoulder which makes our lettering curve to our natural fulcrums.

Write with dark ink. In **Right Tools for the Job,** we touched on this. Whatever you choose to draw with, test your colors for legibility. Only write in those colors.

YELLOW

ORANGE   RED   BLACK

LT. BLUE   BLUE   DK. BLUE

GREEN   PURPLE

PINK   DK. GREEN

                       BROWN

On the previous page, you can see which colors in my palette are legible. I would never use the left column for writing. I may use the center column for large or block letters. I know the right column is always legible and therefore safe to use for lettering.

Applying for a business license, I handed over my application to the clerk at the city office. He carefully studied it and asked, "Did you go to Catholic school?"

I was totally thrown. "Uh, no."

"Are you an engineer?"

I shook my head.

"Then why do you have such good handwriting?"

I laughed, "I write in front of people for a living."

I was happy to meet another person who appreciated good penmanship.

Spelling

Spelling does not need to be daunting. Even if you aren't a great speller, you can more than make up for it in other skills. If you are a great speller, you can still make mistakes.

Again, your audience wants to see you succeed. They are working with you, not against you. When I get publicly called out for misspelling something, which is thankfully rare, I notice the group's response. Most people in the room think the one calling me out is a jerk. People understand what you are writing, despite the mistake.

My favorite cheeky response to making a mistake? A colleague simply drew a red squiggle under the word like a word processing program:

In Practice

Make a disclaimer. If you know you're a bad speller, simply let people know that up front. Then they'll be less distracted by it when you do and you'll feel less pressure when you do.

Ask for corrections—on breaks. Let people know it's alright for them to help you. Ask for them to tell you on break, so they don't disrupt your flow in the moment.

Always pack blank mailing labels. These are your version of correction fluid or the delete button.

Cover up your mistake with mailing labels.

Write your correction over the mailing labels.

Carry a dictionary or a smart phone. You can correct yourself when you have a chance to pause. Be discreet, since using your phone may look like you're checking out instead of checking on spelling.

Write over your writing. This isn't elegant, but it's fast. Write your correction over the word. For instance, protein is one of my tricky words. I always flub the ie or ei. So I may end up writing it one way and then the next over it, like this:

I do this all the time. I cannot remember a time a client has commented on it. In the grand scheme of things, it's minor. Nine out of 10 people are thankful they are not in your position, writing and spelling in front of others.

Work on your spelling. We all have words that trip us up. Two of mine are bureau and entrepreneur. Take the time after a project to learn how to spell them. It will pay off in the long run.

In high school, I was part of a community service organization. In the Spring, we entered a contest making a scrapbook that shared our projects over the year. We went to town on a crazy complicated bus-shaped scrapbook. I was already a block-letter-drawing, drop shadow champ. I drew the final page which read:

Not my finest moment. We didn't win. There's no spell-check on handwriting.

Chart using lettering:

LETTERING
perfectly   drawn
legible   fast

BULLETS
separate   color &
points clear symbol
             coding

COLOR
bright   used to
& inviting organize   LINE

                        connect   thick
                        & contain   & thin

ARROWS
guide   flow &
attention   movement

                    PEOPLE
                            express
                    bring   emotion
                    life to work

        BOXES
highlight   group
& set apart together

                    SHADING
            lift items   add
            off page   dimension

BULLETS

Make separate points clear
Color & symbol coding

Bullets aren't flashy, but they are useful. Sometimes a conversation calls on a long list of items and your fingers will be flying with writing. Bullets help each point stand out from another.

You have plenty of options for style of bullet. It should fit the content you are drawing and be speedy.

In Practice

Separate each point. Use a simple bullet point to make each point clear. You could have a text-filled chart like this:

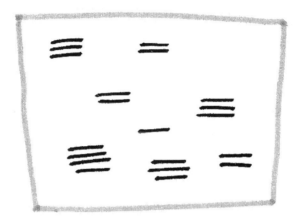

Give each point a bullet to make it clear from a distance:

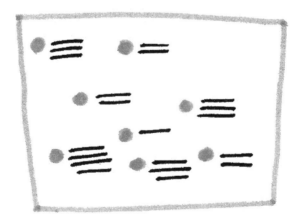

Keep them simple and fast. Remember bullets are fast. They make a point. Don't start with slow, detailed bullets in the beginning. They can slow you down later and get tedious. You can always go back and embellish later if there is a lull in the conversation and the embellishment helps your bullets stand out.

Code with symbols and colors. Perhaps the group is making a list, but there are different qualities within that list. Give yourself simple, differentiated bullets to add meaning:

Most often it can be as simple as good qualities and bad qualities. Only use color or different symbols when it adds to the organization or meaning.

Be consistent. Something as simple as coloring in some bullets, and not others, will distract your audience:

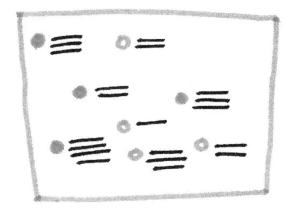

People look for meaning in the differences.

Also, consider consistent placement of your bullets, like the sample above, versus this:

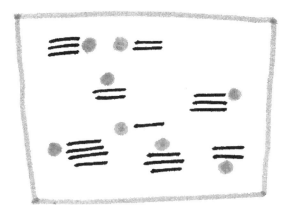

Changing placement is not as distracting as changing color, shape or shading. But consistent placement can be tidier.

Drawing in oval-shaped bullets after a very fast report out. The ovals are yellow and they tie in with the gold coins below Discovery.

Chart using lettering + bullets:

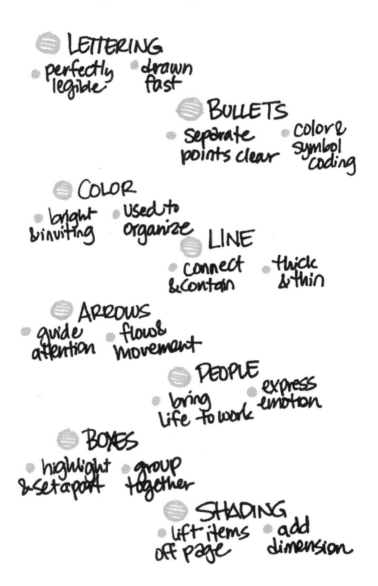

LETTERING
- perfectly legible
- drawn fast

BULLETS
- separate points clear
- color & symbol coding

COLOR
- bright & inviting
- used to organize

LINE
- connect & contain
- thick & thin

ARROWS
- guide attention
- flow & movement

PEOPLE
- bring life to work
- express emotion

BOXES
- highlight & set apart
- group together

SHADING
- lift items off page
- add dimension

COLOR

Bright & inviting
Used to organize

Yes, this is a black-and-white book. Time for your crayons, colored pencils, markers. You are welcome to color in the circles in the following pages to more easily understand the concepts. Crayons and colored pencils are less likely to bleed through the pages than markers might.

Every Mark Has Meaning. The color of every mark has meaning. Make sure you use color in a meaningful way. We will cover the basics of how colors relate to each other. Meaning of color is dependent on your culture and your client.

Let's look at the color wheel.

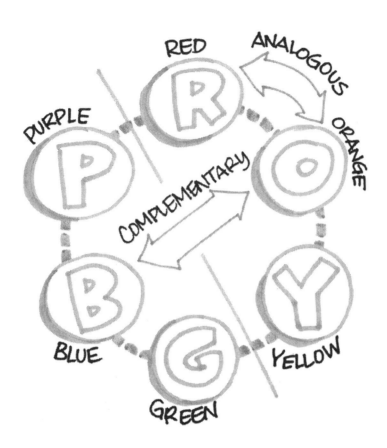

This is your most basic color wheel. Red, yellow and blue are primary colors. Mixing pairs of these primary colors produces the secondary colors of orange, green and purple. Tertiary colors aren't shown on this wheel, but they would be the colors tucked in between these circles, like red-orange and yellow-green.

Red, orange and yellow colors are warm.

Green, blue and purple are cool colors.

Colors across from each other on the color wheel are called complementary colors. These colors are actually quite dynamic and startling when used together. These pairings of orange and blue, yellow and purple, green and red can often be seen in sports uniforms because they catch our eye.

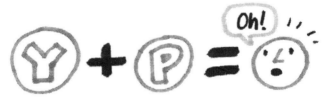

Colors neighboring each other on the color wheel are analogous. These grouping are more calm. We perceive these colors as "going together."

Last, you can have tints and shades of each color (also called hue). You get a tint by adding white to a color. You get a shade by adding black. Dark colors feel closer to you. Light colors recede.

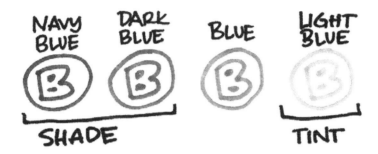

Use tints (light) and shades (dark) for different elements:

used for lines and highlighting, because light colors recede

used for text and drawings, as dark colors are more legible

used for text

I used these three-color groupings in the samples throughout this book. The light colors where a light yellow, dark colors were a gray and a yellow ochre color, along with black. The vast majority of the illustrations in this book where drawn with the same four markers.

To use color to make meaning, the best thing you can do is **limit** your colors. Just because you have every color in the rainbow doesn't mean you should use all of them.

My favorite markers come in a range of 25 colors. I use a palette of 12 colors—usually no more than four colors at one time—one always being black.

Why? Because I want the colors to represent the ideas I'm hearing. For the most part, we're grouping ideas together. You want to use colors that are grouped together.

One chart may be blue, dark blue and black because that chart is all around one question or topic. The next chart may be green, dark green and black because it a different topic from the last chart.

Very Close

Tints and shades of the same color are the closest color grouping. Blue and dark blue match in our minds when we look at them. Using tints and shades of the same color works best for ideas that are very similar to each other.

Close

Analogous colors are near each other in the spectrum. We see these colors as going together. Analogous color schemes (like blue and purple) work well for relating ideas that are similar to each other.

Far Apart

Complementary colors, despite the name, are as opposite in hue as they can be. Put near each other they create a tension. Complementary colors (like blue and orange) can connote two opposite or conflicting ideas.

In Practice

Pick your palette. When choosing your markers, test which markers are tints that recede and which are shades that stand out. Figure out what colors go together and which create visual tension. Create your own palette of colors to choose from.

Be selective. Within your palette, use similar colors to group similar ideas. This is "using color a lot" over "using a lot of colors." Use colors to create organization and meaning.

Understand the culture's colors. Know what colors mean to your audience. If you work within one community, most colors mean the same thing to most people. It is useful to know a company's logo colors alongside their key competitor's. If the company's logo is green, that doesn't mean everything needs to be green. Perhaps you'd create a drawing of their factory in green. Know a school's colors or a city, state or country's flag colors.

Chart using lettering + bullets + color:

LETTERING
- perfectly legible
- drawn fast

BULLETS
- separate points clear
- color & symbol coding

COLOR
- bright & inviting
- used to organize

LINE
- connect & contain
- thick & thin

ARROWS
- guide attention
- flow & movement

PEOPLE
- bring life to work
- express emotion

BOXES
- highlight & set apart
- group together

SHADING
- lift items off page
- add dimension

LINE

Connect & contain ideas
Delineate with thick & thin lines

Different tools make different lines. Most markers fall into these three types of tips or nibs:

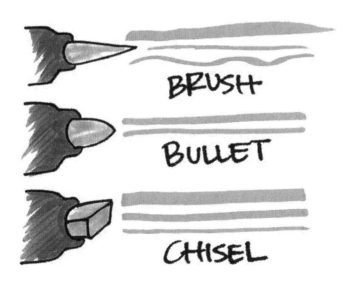

BRUSH

BULLET

CHISEL

Brush tips taper to a fine point and are quite flexible, to mimic a bristled brush. A brush tip's line varies a lot by the pressure you put on the marker. More pressure creates a thicker line; less, a thinner one. The tip's flexibility gives you more gesture and variance in your lines, but less control.

Bullet tips create the most consistent line. The tip is rounded, giving you the same line no matter the angle you hold your marker. Pressure can alter the line slightly. Press down and you'll get a thicker line than if you move a bullet tip lightly and quickly over your paper.

Chisel tips have a combination of options and control. With the shape of a chisel tip, you can hold the pen at three different angles to get three widths of line:

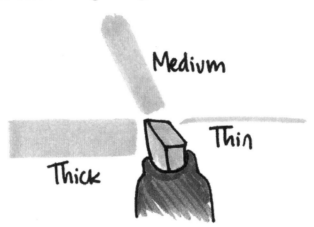

Test different markers to see what amount of control or flexibility suits your working style and the images you are creating.

Use lines to connect, contain, highlight and separate:

Connect ideas to each other. Different thicknesses can signal strong (thick) and weak (thin) ties between ideas.

Enclose an idea in a bubble or box. This sets it apart as a distinct idea. Use light colors for these lines so they don't distract from the text.

Thin, quick lines can separate ideas in a list or a cluster.

Spark lines around an idea or a line under one can highlight the point.

In Practice

Use thick and thin lines to organize. Use dotted, dashed, thin and thick lines to represent different types of connections, from weak to strong.

Weak   **Strong**

Draw confident lines. A tentative drawer makes a simple shape with many small, hesitant lines. The resultant shape is hesitant. Make a shape with a single, bold stroke. Even if that shape is a little wonky, it will have more presence than one made with hesitant marks.

←hesitant   confident→

Using a wide-tip marker to draw a dotted line in between groupings of icons drawn with a narrower chisel tip.

Chart using lettering + bullets + color + line:

1. LETTERING
perfectly legible • drawn fast

2. BULLETS
separate points clear • color & symbol coding

3. COLOR
bright & inviting • used to organize

4. LINE
connect & contain • thick & thin

5. ARROWS
guide attention • flow & movement

6. PEOPLE
bring life to work • express emotion

7. BOXES
highlight & set apart • group together

8. SHADING
lift items off page • add dimension

ARROWS

Guide attention
Create flow & movement

Arrows are the graphic facilitator's best friend. See?

An arrow is a line with a point on one or both ends. Those arrowheads create direction and flow.

We live with arrows everywhere. Next time you are out and about, go on an arrow hunt and see how prevalent they are. They are often used because they are useful. Arrows show us where to go. Use arrows in your charts to show the group where their conversation went. Show the flow of the idea with arrows.

Arrows also represent action. They are great at helping us illustrate processes. Take a look at the arrows on the next page. Jot down your ideas of what you think they could represent. Turn to the following page for some additional answers.

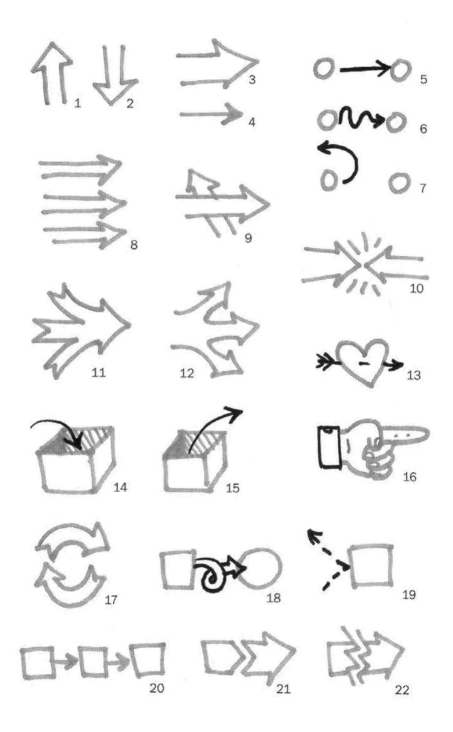

1. Increase, raise, more

2. Decrease, lower, less

3. Strong connection, large movement

4. Weak connection, small movement

5. Direct route or connection

6. Indirect route or connection

7. Off-course, change of route, no connection

8. Alignment, working in parallel

9. Cross purposes, overlap, intersection

10. Conflict, impact, tension, confrontation

11. Convergence, consensus, decision

12. Divergence, generation, multiple choice

13. Love

14. In, contain, enter

15. Out, emerge, exit

16. Point, direction

17. Cycle, feedback

18. Transformation, change

19. Deflect, defend

20. Process, flow

21. Pause, interruption

22. Disruption, discontinuous

Chart using lettering + bullets + color + line + arrows:

Brace Yourself.

It's page 215 and now we start drawing.

Obviously you have been drawings letters, shapes, and making lines. The sixth component is the first that looks like drawing to the casual observer.

Remember that **Content is King** and speed is essential.

Take a deep breath.

Bring life to work
Express emotion

Faces? Star people?

Yes, faces. Yes, star people. When I say essential, I mean essential. Here we talk about the most useful and basic icons. Later, in **Build Your Visual Vocabulary**, we'll go beyond faces and star people. You can get a ton of mileage from simple faces and very simple figures. These help bring character and emotion to all letters, lines, shapes and arrows you're putting on the page.

Meetings are made of people having conversations about what people are currently doing and what they want to be doing. Populate your charts with some people.

Grab a stack of scratch paper and some markers. Fill pages with circles and then start playing with faces. Create your own, unique cast of characters:

Start simple

Work on variations and degrees

Keep building expressions

Turn heads

Add lines for emphasis

Add words

Use symbols

Opposites and contrasts

Work on age range

Build characters with details

And so on, and so on...

Once you've built up an army of simple faces, you can give them simple bodies.

I know stick people get a lot of guff. I'm perfectly fine with you drawing stick people. Easy-to-draw cousins of the stick person are star people, bean people, squiggle people and box-bodied people.

The key to drawing figures is picking the style you enjoy drawing and can adapt to many situations—then sticking to it. As we said in **Make Choices**, be consistent. If you draw three star people and one bean person, your group will wonder where the bean person wandered in from.

Less detail equals more universal when it comes to faces and bodies:

This is a person.   This is a redheaded woman.   This is Kathy from Human Resources.

Some colleagues opt for faceless figures, concentrating on gesture and posture over facial expression. I personally find those drawings detached. I don't want to lose the opportunity to use a range of expression. I want that human connection.

My philosophy is to stick with very iconic figures, unless the group is talking about a specific demographic. I once worked a women's leadership conference—200 women within a giant corporation. I felt like I was in the right room to get more specific with my characterization. On my first chart, I drew three women in the center as a welcoming image:

A woman came up and pointed to the woman who had short hair and asked why I had drawn a man. Sheesh, there were a fair number of women among the 200 who surrounded her with short hair. But that's how our minds work. We look for patterns. We draw conclusions. Long hair = Woman.

Chart using lettering + bullets + color + line + arrows + people:

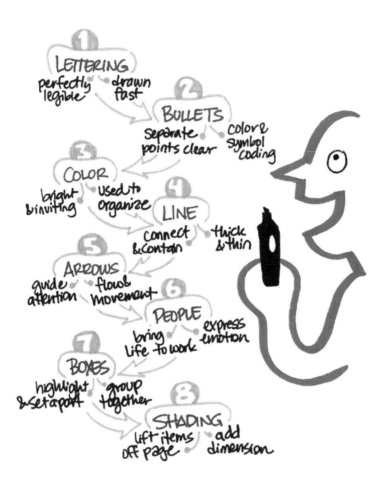

Highlight & sets apart
Group a set of ideas together

Boxes are putting lines around things. Sometimes they aren't boxed-shaped. Boxing an idea sets it apart. Boxing a set of ideas groups them together. A box or shape around an idea makes it feel distinct and complete.

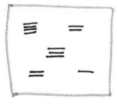 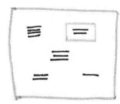 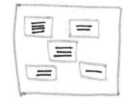

| You can create a chart with five chunks on it. | Perhaps one of those chunks needs to be set apart with a box. | Or all five chunks are of equal importance and you use five boxes. |

The type of shape you use can make the idea feel more concrete, solid, formed—or more amorphous, changeable, abstract:

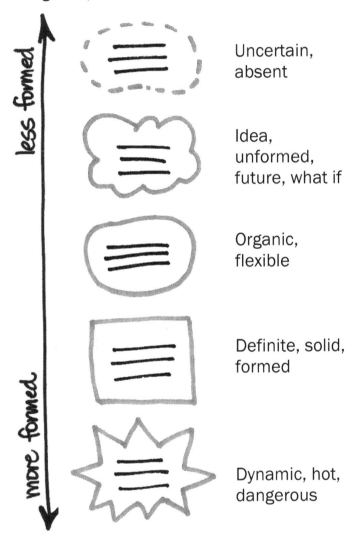

less formed

Uncertain, absent

Idea, unformed, future, what if

Organic, flexible

Definite, solid, formed

more formed

Dynamic, hot, dangerous

In Practice

Content first, box second. It is far, far easier to draw a box around your writing, than try to fit your writing in a box drawn first.

Use a light color. A light line color will help a box recede and not compete with the text it is containing.

Don't become a boxaholic. Boxes are meant to set an idea apart. If you use them for every idea, they lose their meaning and your maps get cluttered.

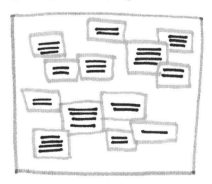

The iconography of this chart is mostly simple figures, boxes and a large banner for the title. This chart is more about thinking and organizing the information spatially, than about drawing a lot of pictures.

Chart using lettering + bullets + color + line + arrows + people + boxes:

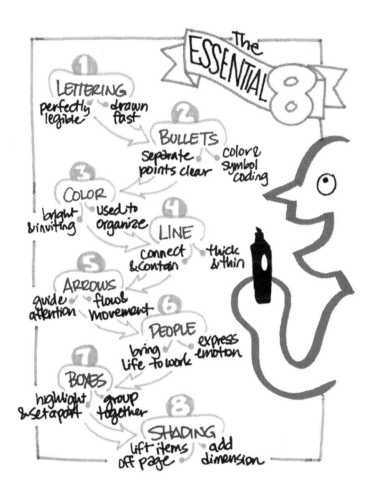

SHADING

Lift items off the page
Add dimension

Shading is a good partner to line. We fill up our charts with tons and tons of lines in the form of letters, shapes, faces, icons and lines themselves:

Shading uses crosshatching, pastels, stippling, or coloring in to make areas of tone, fields of colors. These areas of shading pull focus within a big chart of lines.

Types of Shading

Crosshatching is drawing parallel lines to create a tone. The wider apart and less dense the lines, the lighter the shade. The closer and more dense, the darker the shade.

Instead of lines, **Stippling** uses dots to create tone. Dots can be evenly drawn to create an all-over tone, or can vary to create contour. Stippling is slow and not recommended for graphic facilitation. I use stippling on the 10-Minute Bunny example on page 66.

Fill is making a solid shape completely colored in. You can fill in the shape itself, or create a shape behind the main shape and fill that in to make the white shape pop out.

Contour lines are like crosshatching but they curve to the shape of the object you're drawing.

Shading versus Shadows

No shading or shadow.

Overall shading that colors in a shape, but doesn't make it look three-dimensional.

Shading that makes a shape look three-dimensional.

A drop shadow that makes the shape look like a flat object lifted off the page.

A cast shadow that looks like a light shown on a three-dimensional shape.

Let's say you make a chart like this:

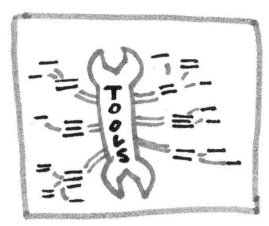

Certainly, there's nothing wrong with it. It uses a central image to anchor the conversation, scale to organize the pieces of information, and lines to connect them.

You could use crosshatching to fill in the central wrench shape to give it more weight on the page:

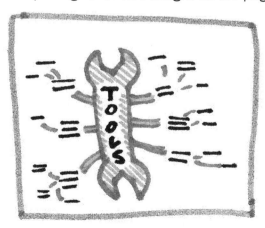

You could also use shading behind the shape, around its edges, to help it look like it's lifted off of the page:

There's no one right way to use shading. But there's one good rule of thumb. You've heard it before. **Be Consistent.**

If you are doing crosshatching, make your lines in a consistent direction. The uniformity of "CROSS" is calming. The variety of "HATCH" is more jumpy, creates more movement. Use uniformity or variety to support the content, but don't be inconsistent. Inconsistency is distracting.

When creating any kind of shadows, imagine where the light source is coming from, and make your shadows consistent to that light source. If you light is coming from the upper right corner, the shadows would fall below and to the left of the letters. The letter A below is inconsistent.

Pastels

A large number of graphic facilitators have pastels among their tools. They are effective at making large areas of tone on paper, or creating more subtle shapes around text.

Chalk pastels are messier than markers. Make sure you don't leave your client's site coated in pastel dust. Also, the dust may compromise the health of your participants. Take heed that pastels don't show up as clearly in photographs as inked lines.

Using pastels to shade a marker-drawn shape

A shape drawn in pastels

Drawing crosshatching to make the outline of a group of people stand out from the background.

Chart using lettering + bullets + color + line + arrows + people + boxes + shading

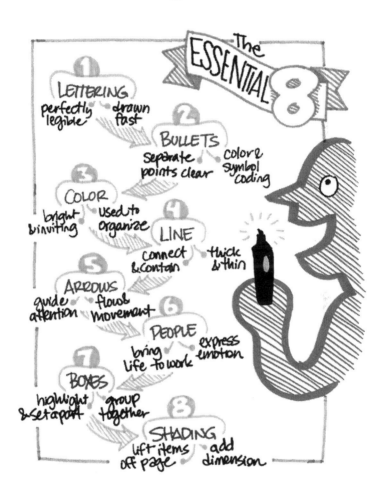

The Silent Ninth Essential: WHITE SPACE

For all the marks you make on your charts, it's the white space that balances them out. White space is the breathing space and it makes what is there clearer.

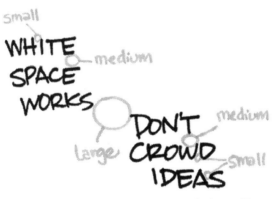

Think of the ninth essential as little pillows that cushion your ideas. You'll use the tiniest pillows between each letter to make them more legible. You use slightly larger pillows between your lines within one chunk of text. Bigger pillows separate one chunk from another. The biggest chunks would buffer one large grouping of ideas from another.

Chart highlighting white space:

Putting It Together

Now, we're going to talk about my Secret Sauce: Synthesis.

Synthesis is about combining pieces from different sources and making something whole—and new—from them. This whole allows you to see the original sources from a different perspective and make new meaning.

As graphic facilitators, we have the opportunity to take all of the individual voices, ideas and comments of a meeting and combine them into a valuable, synthesized map.

It is human nature to make connections and make meaning by combining different sources. We don't often consciously think about this or explicitly make these connections. Few people have learned the tools to record this type of meaning-making in a way that can be built on. Synthesis is very challenging and very rewarding. Your thinking skills and your drawing skills combine to make meaning.

Throughout this book, I've encouraged you to synthesize. In the thinking section, you make connections between things, notice differences and similarities. You **Think in Levels** and sort information into different types. You use anchors and lassos to give groupings of ideas a structure. You find the shape of what is being said.

In the drawing section, you learn how to use visual elements to reinforce the organization of information that you develop in the thinking section. **Every Mark Has Meaning**, and you learn how to use **The Essential Eight** in a meaningful way. You are selective with color and use different colors for different purposes. You make lines of various thicknesses and shapes to create different types of connections between items. You choose when a box will highlight a particular idea and choose when to draw faces and people to give emotion to a comment.

The synthesis seeds planted throughout this book take root in the Principle of **Putting It Together.**

Synthesis goes beyond the basic visual elements or illustration. Here is a concept, snowman, with an illustration of the concept:

SNOWMAN

Synthesis is spatial and shows the structure of what is being said. Seeing the parts, their structure and the whole put together creates more understanding and helps everyone transcend their individual perspectives and create new meaning together. Here are the thinking skills that allow you to synthesize:

A Scan your environment and collect different sources.

B Look for the individual chunks or pieces. Nurture the ability to accurately summarize a piece to its most essential meaning.

not a Snowman   Snowman   Snow bird?   Surprised Snowman   Snow man   Snow ____?

C Look for patterns among the pieces. Compare and contrast to find similarities and differences.

D Group pieces by their type by labeling or classifying the groupings.

E Pull out themes from the pieces.

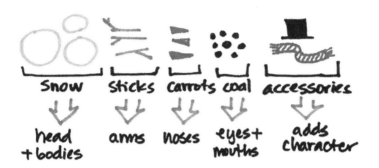

F Make connections between the pieces, showing different types of relationships.

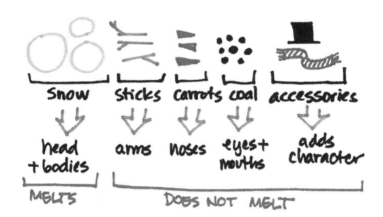

G Make conclusions from the information.

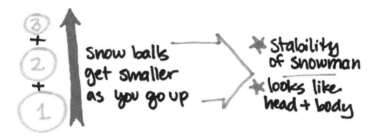

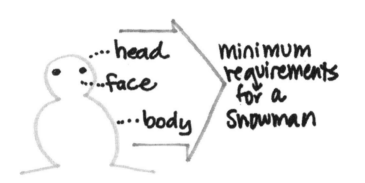

H See the shape of all the pieces together. Show structure.

Arrange the pieces together in an integrated whole. Construct an underlying theory and relate the pieces to that theory.

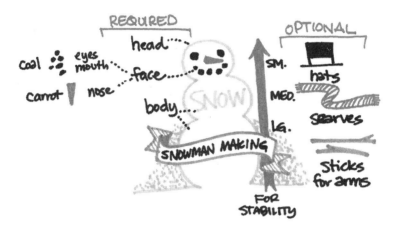

Your ability to synthesize takes you far beyond being able to identify a snowman. You understand how to make the snowman, and the different kinds of snowmen you can make. You can extrapolate this information to make other snow animals.

Go build your snowman!

In the interest of demonstrating how all these elements of synthesis work together, let's use a simple fable as our subject. On the following pages, I will represent this fable five ways, creating a synthesis spectrum.

Stop! Don't turn the page.

Try an experiment. Grab a piece of paper. Read the story to the right. Before you turn the page, make a recording of what you read. There is no right or wrong recording. Give yourself a chance to synthesize the fable. Feel free to reread the fable. Take your time. This is an opportunity to see where you are with synthesis. It is an assessment, not a test.

An Aesop's Fable
The Bundle of Sticks

An old man lay on his deathbed. He summoned his three quarreling sons to give them parting advice. He told the youngest to bring him a bundle of sticks. He handed the middle son the bundle and said, "Break it." The son strained and strained, but with all his efforts, he could not break the bundle. He passed the bundle to the eldest. "Untie the bundle," he said, "And each of you take a stick." When each had done so, he repeated, "Break the stick." Each did so easily. "You see my meaning," said the father.

the End

THE BUNDLE OF STICKS

- Old man, on deathbed
- 3 quarreling sons
- Father → parting advice
- Youngest - "bring me a bundle of sticks"
- Middle - "Break it."
  - ↳ Strained & Strained
  - ↳ could not break
- Oldest - "Untie Bundle"
- Each take stick - "break it"
  - ↳ Easily done
- Father - "You see my meaning."

Stage 1: Listed Text

The fable is represented in text. The text is written in list form, in the same order the story was told.

The text is split into separate pieces and distilled into shorter phrases.

There is a minimum of visual organizing (bullets and a title in uppercase letters). Arrows create flow from one piece of text to the next within one piece of the story.

A lighter color is used for the title and the bullets, helping to differentiate those elements from the text.

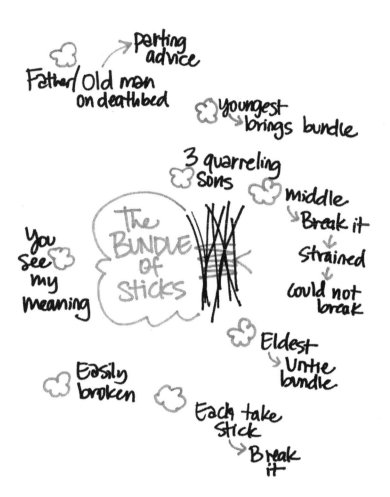

Stage 2: Spatial Text

The text is spread out across the page in a more spatial format, versus the list of Stage 1. It is still primarily in order moving clockwise from the beginning at "Father/Old man on deathbed."

The text is further distilled.

More pictorial bullets are used to separate each point. There are simple arrows used to create connection and flow between some pieces of text.

There is a central focal image of the title with an illustration.

Again, a lighter color is used for the title, arrows and bullets, allowing these elements to recede behind the black text.

Stage 3: Illustrated Spatial Text

Each piece of the story is captured in text, with an accompanying illustration.

This version has more drawn elements, though no flow or structure made explicit through arrows.

The story flows from top to bottom under a banner for the title.

Uppercase letters in a lighter color are used for categorizing labels of "YOUNGEST," "MIDDLE," "OLDEST." Supporting details are written in black lowercase letters.

"NOT BROKEN" and "EASILY DONE" between lighter colored lines set apart two parts of information that are different from the rest. They are both results of the actions of the sons.

Case and color are used to organize the pieces of text.

Stage 4: Structured Spatial Text with Summary Statement

Four quotes from the father are set apart in quote bubbles along with the label of "parting advice."

The structure of story—each son having a role in the story— is reflected in the parallel structure of the bottom half of the page. Each son has the same treatment of a number, label, quote and illustration of his action.

Like Stage 2, the story has a clockwise flow. The flow is made clearer with the dotted line arrows and the numbers.

The old man is illustrated in bed, his context in the story.

The moral of the story, which was not made explicit in the source text, is placed at the close of the circle, "Union gives strength."

Stage 5: Summary Statement

Here, all details of the story itself are absent. The only thing present is the moral of the story.

It is presented with a single image, with more detailed drawing than our previous stages. Crosshatching and solid color are used to create depth within the image.

The meaning of the word "union" is reinforced since it is placed in the ribbon that binds the sticks together.

The Synthesis Spectrum

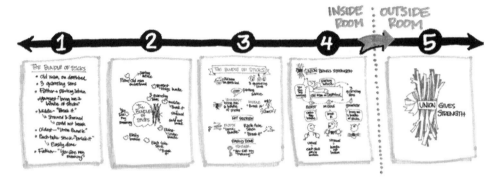

All of these steps are valid recordings of the fable. As we progress, the examples get more sophisticated in their levels of synthesis. The farther to the right we move, the more we see an understanding of the structure of the story and more connections made between the individual pieces.

Contrast between the sons is shown very simply in Stage 3 and made more explicit in Stage 4. The fourth and fifth stages add a conclusion, showing the moral of the story.

We used a fable for our example. Now picture the pieces and structure of this story standing in for the conversation that happens in a meeting.

There is a line dividing stages four and five. Left of the line, you retain the details of the story. This would be the parts of the conversation held in the meeting.

These details are familiar and make sense to those in attendance.

Right of the line, you drop the details and keep only the conclusion. A Stage 5 image could be used as a communication tool to share the conclusion that was reached in the meeting with others who weren't present. The fifth image has a different function than the first four.

In the context of graphic facilitation, it is important to retain the details of the conversation. These recorded details build the shared understanding between the people in the room. The details captured on the map will help participants remember their experience when they see the image after the meeting.

The conclusion, in this case the moral of the story, is a valuable addition to the map. As graphic facilitators we can listen to all the pieces and help the group make meaning, or capture the conclusions the group makes for itself.

Ready for the big finish?

 Like the fable, our strength as graphic facilitators lies in unity. We capture both the sticks and the tie that binds them together.

Ideas are stronger when they are tied together. The pieces of the conversation we map are more meaningful when we find patterns, make connections, show structure and integrate the image into a whole. We bring value when we synthesize the pieces and create something new and more meaningful.

Take a deep breath.

Some of you are humming because the elements of synthesis make sense to you. You already have strong spatial intelligence or the ability to draw conclusions. You feel capable and are happy for the open door into this aspect of the work.

Some of you are gasping, because this all sounds really difficult, impossible even. This doesn't feel natural at all.

It is a spectrum. Yes, I admit I see more value the farther to the right you move. You can serve the group at any of these five stages. You may be a super-detailed person who excels at Stage 1. Your recording may be linear lists, but it gets every detail. You may live in Stage 5, where details feel like a distraction to you, but you love creating summaries that communicate the group's work to a larger audience. You may work in the middle zone.

There are uses for each stage. While I see more value with more synthesis, I work in meetings where the group has a lightning round idea generation. A list of those ideas, Stage 1, is the best output of their process.

The challenge lies in your ability to work at all stages, not be stuck in one or two. This agility will allow you to do your best work and serve your clients well.

In Practice

Assess yourself. After an event, take a look at your charts and see where you would put your work on the spectrum. You will work at different stages for different functions. Ask yourself if the stage you chose was effective for the work at hand. If so, notice what elements made you successful. If not, challenge yourself to improve next time. Practice the elements you missed.

Give yourself time. Harkening back to **Step Back and Listen**, stand quietly and give yourself a chance to listen to synthesize. Pause your drawing and slow down, especially when a group is having an open conversation (versus a single person's presentation or a round of list-making brainstorming).

If you aren't in a live event, give yourself time to think through the sources you're looking at. You can make multiple maps of the information you're working with, using different stages. See what themes arise and what conclusion you make at each stage.

Capture first, make connections second. In a fast-paced conversation, you can get all the details down on the page in text. When there is a lull, you connect and illustrate ideas. The spatial scattering of text in Stage 2 suits this approach. Unlike a list, you can group similar ideas together buffered by white space, making them easier to visually connect later.

Give yourself space. If you are working live, you can give yourself the opportunity to synthesize by giving yourself blank areas to put in themes later. Or hang a flipchart next to your larger chart to capture a synthesis of that work shown side-by-side. While asynchronous to the conversation, these tactics can help add meaning and value. I do favor doing all your work live during the conversation so everyone can see it take place.

Build capacity over time. If you don't come into this work with a strong ability to synthesize, you need to work on it more explicitly. Revisit the actions in the snowman exercise (labeled A through H) and incorporate each into your thinking.

Practice outside of client work. The speed and intensity of our clients' meetings often force us to be on autopilot. Take the initiative to develop these skills outside of your paid projects. You will have more time and space when the stakes are lower. Practice will make your future autopilot mode better and better.

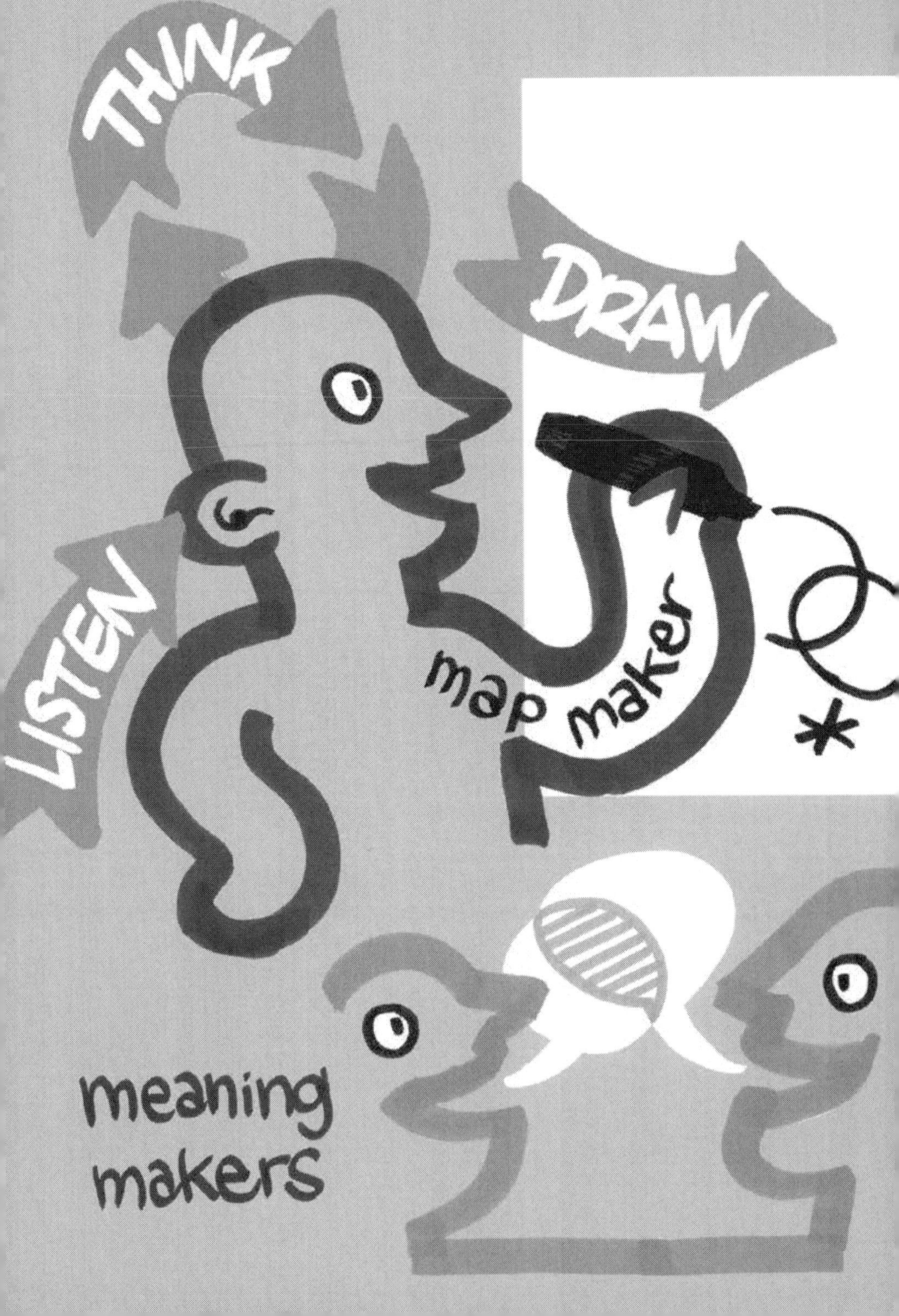
THINK
DRAW
LISTEN
map maker
meaning makers

PRACTICING

Practice Makes Progress

Because facilitation by definition makes work easier, our work looks easy. This effortlessness belies all the practice, experience and adaptability we bring with us.

We tell ourselves "practice makes perfect." Scratch that.

Practice makes ~~perfect.~~ PROGRESS

We are all working to improve our work. We all have off days, and we all have days when we are in the zone. It's practice that helps us progress overall.

You've discovered this work and you're excited. You may feel daunted. The best thing you can do is go out there and do it. Really. It's not any more complicated and I can't make it any simpler. The best way to get your chops is to be bold and work for groups. Hang that giant paper and grab your markers.

Aside from practicing live with groups, you can practice by doing exercises and experiments.

Exercises are doing the same thing over and over to get better at that one function. You can strengthen your drawing skills through simple exercises like fast and furious writing drills. Or practicing icons. The repetition will create muscle memory that will serve you when you work live later.

Experiments are about choosing a specific skill or element and changing it. Take one thing you do consistently and try a new approach. Ask a "what if" question. See what you learn from it. An experiment could be doing a map in only black ink, or just two colors. What if you used a very large marker with a small sheet of paper? What if you listened for the shape of a conversation and wrote no words? What if you worked blindfolded?

You will learn tons from varying your tried and true methods. Yes, I do recommend you leave these for non-client work. Most clients rely on your consistency. Do these experiments on your own time, your own dime.

In Practice

Practice. I know it's obvious. Do it. As suggested in **Succeeding with This Guide**, give yourself the time and space to practice.

Seek a variety of sources. With radio, podcasts and online videos you are never lacking sources to listen to. Observe how different sources produce different maps. For instance, a conversational podcast has a different pace than a highly edited radio piece.

Work live. Take a sketchbook to your next meeting, a talk or a museum visit. Capture what you hear, or make a map of your experience. Ask a friend or colleague who was present for feedback. Be brave and work large and live. It really is the best practice you can get.

Find a mentor. A tipping point in this industry leaves us with far more mentees than mentors. Many experienced people are spending the time in their own business versus advising others. Because of this ratio in the field and my own learning biases as a highly independent introvert, this book encourages you to be self-directed. If you learn best from others, find a mentor, take all the workshops you can and find peers to learn alongside. Respect the time, valuable information and intellectual property your mentors and teachers share with you. Seek many sources and perspectives. Develop your own way of working.

Let your own approach emerge. We will expand on this in the next principle, **Build Your Own Visual Vocabulary**. Many people copy others as a starting point. Instead, let your work come out of your own strengths and experiences. You may have less of an emotional safety blanket, but what you create will be more authentic and truer to you. You will gain the

270

ability to set up your own experiments and learn through observation in a way you wouldn't by aping someone else's work.

Build Your Visual Vocabulary

We each have our own unique way of speaking. Some people are more quiet and reserved, while others command every room. We each have our own vocabulary, favorite phrases, an accent linking us to where we're from. We each have our own voice.

Bring your individual voice to your work as a graphic facilitator. Just as we have our own natural ways of communicating verbally, we have our own ways of communicating visually.

Since many people shut off their drawing switch in childhood, we may be uncomfortable communicating visually. Think of it like learning a second language. You develop competencies through learning and practice. Immersing yourself in a new language speeds up ability more than the occasional class does.

Some of you are very comfortable with visual language. Your challenge is to adapt your fluency to

272

this specific role. You will need to simplify and speed up your ability to draw. To follow this metaphor, you will need to speak in succinct phrases (think of the 10-second bunny) versus a long, detailed paragraph (like the 10-minute bunny).

It is critical to speak your own visual mother tongue. This means developing your own unique style. You can opt to copy someone else's style—the visual equivalent of an American Midwesterner doing a lousy British or Southern accent. It rings false. Better to be honestly and authentically yourself with your misshapen vowels.

I lean heavily on this verbal, word-based metaphor because it is the skill better taught and supported in our culture. Use what you know from your ability to communicate verbally to be a better visual communicator.

 The key is to be yourself and always work to be better. Speak in your visual mother tongue.

Build from the basics in this book. Connect these learnings with what you know in other disciplines. Strengthen your ears, mind and hands through practice. Consciously build your visual vocabulary to be a more fluent graphic facilitator.

In Practice

Build a library. The Essential Eight is just that: essential. You will want to go beyond faces and bodies and simple shapes. Keep a sketchbook to collect iconography, fill a recipe box with cards full of drawings. A smartphone is a fantastic tool. One day I had to draw a mobius strip and was so thankful I could search images in the moment.

Work out ideas by hand. Clip art or photographs are good sources for specific images. Better yet, practice drawing from your sources. For example, taking the time to practice drawing a zebra gives you faster, easier access to drawing one live when your clients start planning their zebra farm. If you bring a photo of a zebra to your project, you'll be slowed down by referring to it while drawing.

Be consistent. Yes, again: Be consistent. In this case consistency is less about reducing confusion for our participants than reducing effort for ourselves. If you frequently draw an image of a bridge to connect two ideas, practice drawing a single bridge over and over.

Then you can effortlessly draw that one bridge anytime you need one. Only if you're working with architects discussing the merits of different bridges will you need more than one.

Be you. Coming from a fine art background, I strongly value originality. This field is still relatively new and there are a few stylistic camps. There is tons of space for new styles. Do something we've never seen before. Do something authentically you. You'll feel better about it and your audiences will appreciate the confidence and honesty in your work.

Use labels. If you draw something clumsily or it's an indistinct image, label it with text. It's no sin.

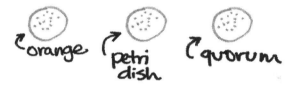

Break up word and image pairings. Not every concept needs an icon. Not every image needs a label. When we borrow our capacity to write and speak to explore this new terrain, we often get locked into a text to picture conversion. When we do, we trap ourselves when we encounter a concept that is difficult to illustrate.

I call this "iconitis." You can see it in **Putting It Together**'s Stage 3 fable example on page 254. Iconitis is when your icons are inflamed. No—it's when you get caught up in having an icon for each and every idea, and you're unable to use imagery beyond this function. A chart could have a field of drawings all the same size. The chart looks visual and inviting, but these icons aren't being used to create more meaning or to organize the information.

Curb client-specific imagery. In **Process over Product**, you were invited to prepare yourself for a specific client by drawing their products. For example, drawing apples and bananas to prepare for working for a produce company. Do it to help yourself feel prepared. But be open to the needs of your client, not what you want to draw. Your produce company folks will likely be talking about distribution (trucks, ships) or human resources (people), not specifically bananas.

Mind your motifs and metaphors. Your client mentions a rocket ship launching to reach a planet of a goal. It's an enticing visual. You could take flight with the metaphor and draw charts full of stars and solar systems. You could have tons of fun drawing astronauts. Be careful to keep yourself grounded. Don't let exciting metaphors or motifs pull you out of the conversation. Use imagery but always keep it in alignment with the conversation. Use metaphors that are created and fostered by the group.

Build your visual vocabulary from concepts, not icons. Instead of giving you pictures to copy, the following page contains something more valuable. Page 278 is a list of common concepts discussed in meetings. Develop your own imagery to support these ideas. Not all concepts lend themselves to imagery. Come up with a few ideas for each concept. Different icons can be useful for different scenarios or company cultures.

Common Meeting Concepts

balance

capacity

change

collaboration

commitment

communication

connection

culture

customers, users, patients, consumers

data, databases

direction

diversity and inclusion

feedback

finance

focus

goals

growth

infrastructure

innovation

insights, key learnings

integration

labor

leaders, leadership

local vs. global

management

metrics

models

organizations

participation, engagement

passion

performance

planning

quality

resources

retention

rewards

strategy

support

sustainability

time, timeframes, short-term, long-term

tools

training, education

transformation

values

vision

*Sharing my iconography in a workshop. These simple drawings represent 90% of the pictures I draw on client projects. The dozen participants were incredulous; this really is what I draw. What makes me **me** is how I use scale and synthesis with these simple images.*

Challenge Yourself

We are nearly always the only graphic facilitator in the room. You may not get much chance to work with colleagues. We won't get direction, criticism or advice from others because our clients don't have the context and understanding to challenge us. We need to challenge ourselves.

This work is still brand-new to most people. You will get lots and lots of "oohs and aahs" from people. Praise is great. Praise encourages us. But we also need to be self-critical. Since most clients and participants have no previous experience, you are unlikely to get detailed feedback from them.

It is important to be self-aware, able to diagnose problems, and ready to recognize your progress. You are the one person in the best position to do that.

In Practice

Record the conversation. With consent from your client, you can record audio our video of your work. After the event, you can replay audio and see how well you captured the content of the meeting. With video, you can also notice your body language.

Check in with your client. Often we can't take a lot of our client's time during an event. Quickly asking, "Anything I should be doing differently?" may spark a course correction. Generally checking in with the facilitator can open up channels of communication. Sharing a useful observation about how the group is progressing can invite your client to check in with you, too.

Write yourself notes. If you notice you did something wrong, or got flustered, make a quick note of the issue. Don't dwell, don't derail yourself, simply get it down on paper. You can reflect on your note later and remember how to improve next time. This work is intense and in-the-moment. After the event, you are on to the next project. A simple *Note to Self* can help you make improvements.

Create a cohort. While most of our projects are solo, you can always create a group of peers to compare notes with, share stories and network together. Again, the demand for mentors is larger than the supply among graphic facilitators. Turn to your peers to share knowledge and challenge each other.

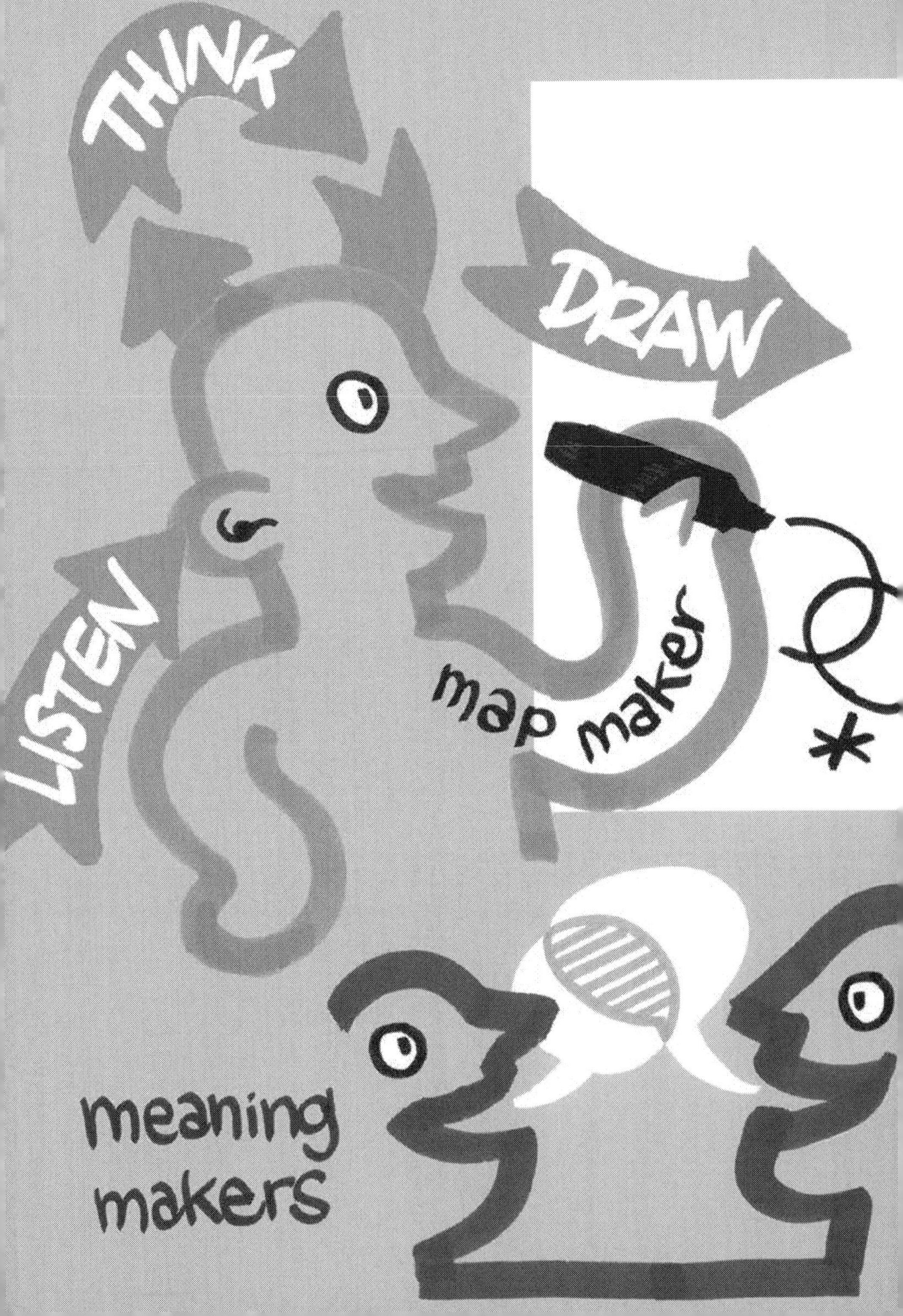
THINK
DRAW
LISTEN
map maker
meaning makers

Your Presence is Powerful

The powers of graphic facilitation are: The **Power of Being Listened To**, the **Power of Shared Understanding** and the **Power of Seeing and Touching Your Work**. These are incredibly empowering factors in a meeting. As the graphic facilitator, you are the human representation of these powers. **Your Presence is Powerful.**

The way you carry yourself in a meeting at the front of the room has an impact. Yes, you are a powerful presence. And as we said early on, **It's Not About You**. There is a balance to strike between the ninja and the showman.

On one side are the ninjas who want to disappear into the paper. They never face the group. Their body language is so stealth the group forgets they are there. At worst, the ninja can be seen as cowering and subservient. On the other side of the spectrum are the showmen, who make their work a performance. They pull more focus to themselves than their maps. At worst, the showmen are bombastic and attention-grabbing.

It is entirely your choice when it comes to how you carry yourself in the room. You set the expectations with your client. I feel the sweet spot is in the middle, where you are participating and present, neither disappearing nor distracting. Be present and be an equal partner to the group.

Your whole body communicates. Your demeanor and personality communicates. Be aware of how you are communicating to the group through your body language.

In Practice

Be introduced. From **It's Not About You**, this is worth repeating. From the start, everyone should know your name and how you are there to help. As outsiders, folks forget to make us nametags. Make your own. As people enter the room and try to place your unfamiliar face, introduce yourself.

Be still. Even if you are nervous or you are picking up on the tension in a group, do not fidget or pace. You will distract the group. When you **Stop and Listen**, find a still standing stance that is comfortable for you.

Manage your energy. Graphic facilitation is taxing work. We stand much of the day; we are stretching to reach up and draw. You need to manage your own energy to meet the demands of the meeting. Wear appropriate clothes and shoes for standing and stretching. Stretch and bend your knees during breaks. Keep yourself fed and hydrated. Get rest before and after projects.

Sit down when appropriate. If the group is 90 minutes into a scheduled 40-minute conversation, you may be tired and want to sit. Notice the focus of the group; often your sitting down while a group is keyed up may downshift the room's energy. When a group is in the thick of conversation, it is better to keep standing to stay present with them.

Dress the part. You need to balance your clothing to both be comfortable for the work you are doing, and blend in with the group you are helping. If you are working with a room full of people in three-piece suits, they will understand that it's hard to tape a huge sheet of paper to the wall wearing a tailored blazer. Wear clothing that lets you stretch and squat. Wear shoes appropriate for standing most of the day. I suggest no loud prints to distract the group from your work, since you are often standing in front of your drawing.

Interact with the group. Even though we are usually outsiders, you don't have to be a stranger. On breaks, answer questions people have. Accept compliments graciously. While you are performing a role that is new and may be alien to many, you are a human being working with other human beings.

Retreat and recharge. Given the intensity of this work, make sure you get the mental and physical breaks you need to pace yourself. I'm an introvert, so I tend to decline lunch table invitations or offers to join the group off hours. I'm thankful my clients want to include me, but opt out so I can get a little quiet solo time to reset for the next segment of the meeting.

Accept help. If someone wants to help you move a chart or tape up your paper, let them. In general, we need to be self-sufficient, but take help when offered. If someone points out a mistake or something you missed, graciously accept corrections. They know you are there to help them; they are on your side. There is no need to get flustered or feel defensive.

Eighty people were in a plenary conversation. It was chugging along at a great pace. I was drawing, drawing, drawing. Then they stalled. I stood back, facing the group, calmly listening and watching. Conversation continued but they weren't making progress. They weren't saying anything that wasn't already up on the wall.

Finally a man piped up, pointing to me: "Have you noticed she hasn't drawn anything for the last 20 minutes? We're not getting anywhere."

His observation jolted the group into progress again. I'm so glad he used me to demonstrate that the group was stalled. I could have been a busy bee, rewording and rewriting the same stuff they already said. That would not have served the group. It would have cluttered up the board and used up space could be filled with new ideas.

Partner Up

We have focused on graphic facilitation alone. It is important to learn how to work independently, since in some events we get little direction.

We are often partnered in events with facilitators. Or working with a client who is taking on the facilitator role within their meeting. At conferences, you are likely to be introduced by an emcee and be working out your logistics with a production company running the conference. These partnerships run the gamut from vital to vexing.

You can be brought in from the start of a project, co-designing an agenda with a facilitator. You can be practically parachuted in at the last minute with your paper and markers. You need to discover your best ways of working or how you can adapt to the given situation.

In Practice

Describe your ways of working and what you deliver. Set expectations up front. As you describe what you do in person and as you write your marketing materials, describe the way you like to work. If you love co-creating meetings from scratch, tell people. You will attract that work. If you have a fantastic, unique deliverable, make that crystal-clear. Let people know how you work best. Hiring a graphic facilitator is still very new to most folks. Anything you share about your process will help them determine if you are the right partner for them.

Be ready for anything. Adaptability is the number one skill in graphic facilitation. Over time, you will learn your preferred ways of working. Over time, you will learn that anything can happen and will. Agendas change. Logistics change. I have corresponded and contracted with a person for weeks, only to find out they aren't my client—just the person tasked to find one of those graphic facilitator people.

You need to be ready to contribute with little or no direction. Many of your clients haven't worked with a graphic facilitator before, so you need to take the lead.

I have shown up for projects where I realized no one really understood why on Earth I was there. I also have a few facilitators I've worked with for over a decade; we now practically communicate telepathically. I have had facilitators collaborate with me, while others have ignored me. I know that I have to make the most of my role for the benefit of the group, no matter what the dynamics are between the clients, facilitators and me. I am there to serve the participants.

Understand your multiple clients. Fundamentally, we serve the whole group in the meeting. And we serve different clients. The facilitator we work with is one client. The facilitator's client is another. Often, our client's boss becomes another client. Being able to read and navigate these different clients is vital to our role as facilitators. If you are a subcontractor for a facilitator or a client, respect that you are representing their company, not your own.

Speak up for your visual skills and tools. With all these layers of clients and shifting agendas, you can get lost in the shuffle. If you see your work being compromised, speak up. For instance, if you find you are literally being put in a dark, remote corner, speak up and tell your client you need to be seen to have an impact. If you see an opportunity for the group to better engage with your work, let your client know that. Facilitators and clients have their own skills and strengths, but you are likely the only person in the room tuned in to the visual tools in the room.

Give them the Markers

As you strengthen your own skills through your work as a graphic facilitator, you'll see how useful and powerful it is to empower others to expand their own capacities to listen, think and draw.

You will find yourself sharing your markers.

While you are absolutely there to fill the role of graphic facilitator, in some parts of some meetings with some processes, it is best that the participants draw and write out their ideas.

Giving people instruction to draw in the presence of a professional can be intimidating. You have many ways to empower participants to pick up the pen.

In Practice

Give everyone the right tools. Make sure that the safest and most legible materials are on hand for the exercise. If you have flipchart paper, make sure you have loads of fresh markers on hand, and no whiteboard markers. If you want people to share sticky notes with the group, give them thicker tipped markers that result in more legible writing, not ballpoint pens.

Give everyone good examples. When you instruct your group to participate, give them clear instructions and examples. If you want each team to write out five sticky notes, post mock sticky note examples written in the pens you give them and with clear handwriting. Clear examples help the groups better understand what's expected of them, and they will deliver.

Say no. I do believe in service. One time I say no to clients is when they need to serve themselves. In many meetings we work in one, big plenary group and then split off into smaller breakout groups. Often in that transition a participant may ask, "Can we have Brandy?"

I say no. While it's awkward if the client or facilitator feels I'm always on the clock, I am not trying to get out of work. The small group needs to listen to each other and think and draw out their own ideas together. When I used to accept these requests, I very often became their crutch. These groups need to be doing their work for themselves.

I gently say no by saying, "I can't commit to one group, but if you need help with a small, specific task, I'm here for everyone."

Walk the walk. If you give instruction, be the first to follow it. This is rarely a problem for graphic facilitators because it's hard for us to click out of our mode of working. Encourage the facilitators and clients you partner with to model the behaviors you want. A facilitator who off-handedly says, "Oh, I don't draw, Brandy does," has just given every person in the room permission to give up. We model the behaviors we want to see.

Watch what you reward. Because **Content is King,** always, always reward substance over style. People are nervous about their drawing skills, so people will often compliment each other's borders of flowers or penmanship. Both are fine and dandy, but what ideas are being shared? What work is being done? Always reward messy but meaningful work over pretty and empty work. We all deserve gold stars for good work— as long as it is good work toward the task at hand.

Now, Go Do Great Work!

I am so thankful to share my thinking about graphic facilitation with you. I believe the Powers of this works are great and I hope the Principles will guide you to do great work for yourself and with your clients. I hope I was able to break down all those skills I listed way back on page 12 into understandable, adoptable and adaptable pieces so you can assemble and develop your skills. Graphic facilitation will help you serve a group and its work in a way few people can. I hope you find the practice of listening, thinking and drawing to make meaning as gratifying as I do.

Do it to it. Get out there and try your hand at the work. You may have found a fantastic tool that helps you and the groups you serve do great work—whether you are the graphic facilitator or bring these skills into other roles. You may not love graphic facilitation. The only way to know is to try.

Tag it and share it. Use the tags in the headers, described on page 31, to share your use of these principles with others.

Visit GraphicFacilitator.com. Click on over to my site where you will find resources and see the conversation around the book. Find out what new things I've cooked up to help you work visually.

Draw on! Enjoy. Have fun. Graphic facilitation is incredibly rewarding work. I wish you great opportunity, fine-tuned ears, a clear mind and nimble fingers!